PRAISE FOR *RUNAWAY EMOTIONS*

"Emotions are a powerful part of our lives, but often they are the least understood. Jeff Schreve's *Runaway Emotions* offers the help we need for hearing the 'deeper messages' our emotions are telling us and how to enlist God's help in addressing them. I highly recommend it."

ROBERT LEWIS, PASTOR AND FOUNDER, MEN'S FRATERNITY

"Jeff Schreve understands both the devastating consequences and powerful influences of human emotions. No matter what you may be struggling with, there is real help in these insightful pages. Don't miss this very practical and helpful book."

DR. ED HINDSON, DISTINGUISHED PROFESSOR,
SCHOOL OF RELIGION, LIBERTY UNIVERSITY

"Most people don't suffer from a lack of IQ, instead their main deficit is a poor EQ (Emotional Quotient). Jeff Schreve gives us a primer on how to better understand emotions—your own and those of friends and family members. If you want to grow your EQ Jeff will equip you to do just that in fresh and practical way."

DR. DENNIS RAINEY, CEO, FAMILYLIFE MINISTRIES

"Dr. Martin Lloyd Jones famously said that most of our unhappiness in life is due to the fact that we spend more time listening to ourselves than in talking to ourselves. The Bible refers to this idea as 'taking every thought captive.' My friend Jeff Schreve wants to help us learn how to *take every feeling captive*, and many Christians in our day need to learn just how to do that."

BOB LEPINE, RADIO CO-HOST, FAMILYLIFE TODAY

"As a psychologist, I take a special interest in books dealing with emotional health. In *Runaway Emotions*, Jeff Schreve provides key insights that will help you turn negative emotions into positive results."

DR. CHARLES LOWERY, PRESIDENT AND CEO, LOWERY
INSTITUTE FOR EXCELLENCE, INC.

"This book will make your heart sing with joy! Pastor Jeff Schreve helps us to identify those negative emotions we have all experienced. But the book doesn't end there. *Runaway Emotions* reveals the overcoming hope we have in Christ--the hope that takes us from bound up to breaking free!"

BABBIE MASON, SINGER-SONGWRITER AND

AUTHOR, WWW.BABBIE.COM

"Every pastor has run the gamut of dealing with people whose emotions have stepped into the path, derailing logic, but worse still, derailing the counsel of the Word of God. Jeff Schreve, a gifted pastor and preacher, now provides a way to walk through these emotions and return to the sage advice of God's Word."

PAIGE PATTERSON, PRESIDENT, SOUTHWESTERN BAPTIST

THEOLOGICAL SEMINARY, FORT WORTH, TX

RUNAWAY
EMOTIONS

Why You Feel the Way You Do
and What God Wants You to Do About It

JEFF SCHREVE

THOMAS NELSON
Since 1798

NASHVILLE   DALLAS   MEXICO CITY   RIO DE JANEIRO

Published in Nashville, Tennessee, by Thomas Nelson. Thomas Nelson is a registered trademark of Thomas Nelson, Inc.

Thomas Nelson, Inc., titles may be purchased in bulk for educational, business, fund-raising, or sales promotional use. For information, please e-mail SpecialMarkets@ThomasNelson.com.

Unless otherwise indicated, Scripture quotations are taken from the NEW AMERICAN STANDARD BIBLE®, © 1960, 1962, 1963, 1968, 1971, 1972, 1973, 1975, 1977, 1995 by The Lockman Foundation. Used by permission.

Scripture quotations marked AMP are taken from THE AMPLIFIED BIBLE: OLD TESTAMENT. ©1962, 1964 by Zondervan (used by permission); and from THE AMPLIFIED BIBLE: NEW TESTAMENT. © 1958 by the Lockman Foundation (used by permission). Scripture quotations marked CEV are taken from THE CONTEMPORARY ENGLISH VERSION. © 1991 by the American Bible Society. Used by permission. Scripture quotations marked ESV are taken from THE ENGLISH STANDARD VERSION. © 2001 by Crossway Bibles, a division of Good News Publishers. Scripture quotations marked GNT are taken from THE GOOD NEWS TRANSLATION. © 1976, 1992 by The American Bible Society. Used by permission. All rights reserved. Scripture quotations marked KJV are taken from The Holy Bible, King James Version (public domain). Scripture quotations marked TLB are taken from *The Living Bible.* © 1971. Used by permission of Tyndale House Publishers, Inc., Wheaton, Illinois 60189. All rights reserved. Scripture quotations marked NIV are taken from the Holy Bible, New International Version®, NIV. Copyright © 1973, 1978, 1984, 2011 by Biblica, Inc.™ Used by permission of Zondervan. All rights reserved worldwide. www.zondervan.com. Scripture quotations marked NKJV are taken from THE NEW KING JAMES VERSION. © 1982 by Thomas Nelson, Inc. Used by permission. All rights reserved. Scripture quotations marked NLT are taken from the Blue Letter Bible, *New Living Translation.* © 1996, 2004, 2007 by Tyndale House Foundation. Used by permission of Tyndale House Publishers, Inc., Carol Stream, Illinois 60188. All rights reserved. Scripture quotations marked PHILLIPS are taken from J. B. Phillips: THE NEW TESTAMENT IN MODERN ENGLISH, Revised Edition. © J. B. Phillips 1958, 1960, 1972. Used by permission of Macmillan Publishing Co., Inc. Also quoted: *The Message* by Eugene H. Peterson. © 1993, 1994, 1995, 1996, 2000. Used by permission of NavPress Publishing Group. All rights reserved.

Library of Congress Cataloging-in-Publication Data

Schreve, Jeff, 1962-
 Runaway emotions : why you feel the way you do and what God wants you to do about it / Jeff Schreve.
  p. cm
 Includes bibliographical references.
 ISBN 978-1-4002-0482-3
 1. Emotions--Religious aspects--Christianity. I. Title.
 BV4597.3.S38 2013
 248.8'6--dc23
                                    2012043570

Printed in the United States of America

13 14 15 16 17 RRD 6 5 4 3 2 1

CONTENTS

FOREWORD

It is a special delight to me to see Jeff Schreve's book, *Runaway Emotions*, be made available for the many who are interested in the ebb and flow of their emotions. In a way, it is an extension of my own pilgrimage, and my pursuit of answers more consistent with biblical principles.

After studying counseling in graduate school and serving as a pastor for two decades, I wrote *The Message in Your Emotions* in 1996. My wife, Sharon, and I had been in the process of sorting out our own psychological journeys for several years. We had both come from what are now called *dysfunctional* families. Our fathers were both alcoholics. We were both firstborn. These factors and others contributed to an interesting mixture of shared hang-ups. I wanted to figure us out and to help others understand themselves.

My efforts to find a workable counseling method were based on two assumptions. First, I believed that the nature of man, like the rest of creation, was reasonable and understandable. There are patterns to God's creative work. There is a design. So I made notes, recording observations on the wonderful variety of emotions we experience, particularly the painful ones. Somewhere there was a clear trail back to the source of our troublesome feelings.

My second assumption was that the wisdom of biblical principles held answers for emotional distress. I accepted the Bible as authoritative and completely trustworthy and believed there were timeless truths revealed in its laws, history, letters, sermons, and stories. If we could get past legalism on the one hand and skepticism on the other, we could identify universal principles to help us understand the mystery of our emotions.

I had no pretensions that this model for self-understanding would end the search. But I knew that God created us in His own likeness, with finite qualities like His infinite ones. Each of those qualities comes with inherent desires that are part of our being human. In the book I presented an interpretation of negative emotions as a warning system that one of these desires is threatened.

Jeff Schreve is a gifted communicator. He is also gifted at seeing through the clutter of our human thought and emotions to the answers we need. He was a student of mine years ago at Southeastern Seminary. I recognized his gifting even then.

While at Southeastern, Jeff took a course with me, based on the material in *The Message in Your Emotions*. Years later, he preached a series of compelling sermons on those basic ideas. He did a marvelous job of making his sermons expositional with a careful study of biblical texts as the basis for each message. I heard him preach from that series in his church in Texarkana. The message had a depth that really caused me to think. It had humor and word pictures that kept my attention. But mostly it was true to the Bible on the one hand and to our experience as human strugglers on the other.

I will not soon forget the smoke alarm Jeff had with him at the pulpit. As he described the emotional warning system God has built into our nature, he pressed the button and sent the shrill sound of the alarm through the auditorium. Those of us in the audience jumped and then laughed nervously. He had us. We got the point.

As he continued to explain and apply the principles from his text, we couldn't have stopped listening if we had tried.

What Jeff has written in *Runaway Emotions* came from that series of sermons. He began with some of the ideas we studied years ago when he was a student. But now he has made them more profound, more true to life, and more understandable. This book will open your eyes to the mystery of your own painful emotions. It will help you not only to sort out your own feelings but also to help others who are confused about why they feel the way they do.

So get comfortable and prepare yourself for an adventure of self-discovery. With it you will also find a new joy in the mercy and grace of God. He created us. He understands us. He wants us to understand ourselves and adjust our lives to His intentions for us. He wants us to see the place of our troublesome emotions in that process.

WAYNE McDILL,
WAKE FOREST, NORTH CAROLINA

INTRODUCTION

Emotions. They really make life fun and exciting, don't they? Can you imagine how boring life would be if God had never created emotions?

One of my all-time favorite TV characters was Mr. Spock of *Star Trek* fame. Spock, as you may remember, was a pointy-eared alien from the planet Vulcan. As was the case with all Vulcans, he had learned from his earliest days to suppress any display of emotion, even to the point of denying that he had any emotions at all.

The trouble was Mr. Spock had a human mother, and because he was half human, those pesky human emotions might emerge at the most inconvenient moments. Most of the time, however, the only reaction you'd get out of Spock would be the raising of a single eyebrow, coupled with the word, "Fascinating!"[1]

To the contrary, life without emotions would not be fascinating in the least. Why? Because emotions make life worth living. They bring spice and flair to the human experience.

Emotions truly are the colors of life. Without them, we're only two-dimensional shades of gray. Musician Jan Hammer once noted, "Emotions are the fuel to really move you along. That's the only way you can create music. If you don't feel any emotions, it's not going to happen."[2]

Unfortunately, as fallen human beings living in a fallen world, we aren't given the privilege to pick and choose which emotions we will experience in our lives. We appreciate and value all the joy, love, laughter, peace, and wonder we can wrap our arms around. But then . . . we also have to deal with the dark side of the emotional spectrum. There we find fear, worry, anger, and bitterness. Guilt, loneliness, and embarrassment also join in to rear their ugly heads. Most of us would rather not have to experience those sorts of emotions, and we really don't like it when negative emotions run away with our joy and peace. But as I've said, we have to deal with life as it comes, and we don't get to avoid all of those unpleasant feelings this side of heaven.

But even those emotions—the darker and more difficult ones— are important. In fact, they reveal a great deal about who we are and where we are in life.

Two Types of Smoke Alarms

When I preached a series on this subject at my church, I stood in front of the congregation with a small, plastic device in my hands. People in the last couple of rows may not have been able to figure out just what it was.

They figured it out immediately after I pushed a little button.

Suddenly, the auditorium filled with that familiar, shrill, ear-splitting sound—the alarm of a smoke detector. While some may not have liked that particular audiovisual aid, everyone was certainly awake for it!

Most of us have smoke detectors—several of them—in our homes. (If you don't, you should.) They come in different shapes, sizes, and colors, of course, but none of them is particularly attractive.

Right? Who walks into your home, looks up at the ceiling, and says, "Wow. Nice smoke detector. Where can I get one like that?"

No, they're not particularly attractive. But they certainly have a purpose. A shrilling smoke alarm in the middle of the night says, "Wake up! There is trouble! Something is on fire!" That alarm may save our very lives someday.

It's my premise in the pages ahead that God allows negative, runaway emotions to permeate our souls for a reason. Those uncomfortable, undesirable feelings, like the ones I've listed in the table of contents, have a strong purpose in our lives. They, too, serve as warning bells, or alarms. They tell us, *There's a problem here. Wake up! Something's wrong. Something's out of adjustment. Something desperately needs attention. We've got a fire here, and you need to do something about it!*

> *Those uncomfortable, undesirable feelings have a strong purpose in our lives. They serve as warning bells.*

Understanding Your "Smoke Alarm"

When I was in seminary, I took an "I Term" class ("I" stands for intensive) over Christmas break on the subject of emotions. My teacher, Dr. Wayne McDill, opened my eyes to the positive role that negative emotions can play in our lives. He impressed upon me the idea that God has a use for those unhappy, darker emotions that cast their occasional shadows across our lives. In fact, God has a message for us in those feelings, if we would only open our ears (and hearts) to receive it.

Concerning this subject, Dr. McDill said,

One of the primary clues a physician uses to discover what is ailing you is to ask, "Where does it hurt?" God has built a marvelous warning system into our physical makeup. When we feel pain, we know something is wrong. Like a siren going off in our minds, pain or discomfort sends us to the immediate aid of a hurt finger, sick stomach, or throbbing tooth. We don't ignore these signals. They are persistent in getting our attention.

Emotional pain is also normal. It is a warning that something is out of order, that some nonphysical injury or disease threatens you. You may feel just a little loneliness, a bit of anger, a mild frustration, or you could experience more serious and ongoing suffering. Either way, the alarm is designed to get your attention, to send you a message about a threat in some area of your life. There is a message in your emotions.

Yes, there is! A specific and compelling message can be found in each of your negative, painful emotions.

Dr. McDill inspired me to pursue that theme in the book you hold in your hands. He has been excited about this subject for many years and is thrilled to see this life-changing concept reach the largest number of people. I presented the truths of this eye-opening work in a series of messages at my church in Texarkana, Texas. This book is based on those messages.

And Dr. McDill is happy to see the book come to print. He has collaborated with me throughout the writing process and believes God will use this work to touch lives and really help people discover why they feel the way they do . . . and what God wants them to do about it.

So, with thanks to my wise and perceptive friend Wayne McDill, I encourage you to explore with me the potentially *positive* impact of those troublesome *negative* emotions that you'd prefer to discard. In fact, I urge you to listen to the shrilling of the smoke alarm of your painful emotions, *and do something about it.* Ripping out the battery or clipping the wires won't do anything to solve the deeper problem and bring healing. The truth is, God Himself is trying to speak to you through those emotions— right now. He wants to show you exactly what is wrong so you can effectively deal with the source of the problem, and not waste time masking the symptoms.

God wants to show you exactly what is wrong so you can effectively deal with the source of the problem, and not waste time masking the symptoms.

So, if you are ready to put out some fires within and silence the smoke alarm of your painful, runaway emotions, turn the page and let's get started.

ONE

EMBARRASSMENT

When You Feel Inferior

But I am no longer a human being; I am a worm, despised and scorned by everyone! All who see me make fun of me; they stick out their tongues and shake their heads.

I have always been uncomfortable and insecure with public speaking. That's quite an admission for a preacher and someone who speaks for a living, but it's true.

Still, I can't help wondering if my nervousness has been a blessing in disguise through the years. The Lord knows how very dependent I am on His strength and help every time I stand up to speak. I'm not sure I could begin to describe how many times He has put confidence into my voice as I've opened my Bible and looked out across a sea of expectant faces week after week.

Back in college, however, I hadn't yet experienced God's grace and enabling in this area of my life, and my fear was intense. My idea had been to tiptoe into public speaking a little at a time during my four years in college at the University of Texas—as you might wade into the shallow end of a cold swimming pool inch by inch. However, the college department director at our church in Austin had other ideas. Everett Sheffey meant to throw me in the deep end to see if I could swim!

Everett chose me to be the student leader one year, which meant doing opening announcements every Sunday morning in front of a couple hundred students. *Horrors!* To make matters worse, he wouldn't take my emphatic "NO!" for an answer.

My big debut was in January 1982, at the beginning of the spring semester. Wouldn't you know it, the place was packed. My friend and former student leader and announcement guy, Shawn, was visiting that Sunday. He had done a marvelous job as leader, and I admired him greatly.

Beth, a really sweet girl who knew I was nervous about speaking, was also in the audience that day. That morning she had given me a scripture to encourage my heart and calm my fears: "Have I not commanded you? Be strong and courageous! Do not tremble or be dismayed, for the LORD your God is with you wherever you go" (Josh. 1:9). I was clinging to that verse as I reviewed the announcements I was to share that morning.

How nervous was I? Believe it or not, I could actually see the end of my tie bouncing up and down on my shirt, in rhythm with my racing heart.

Shawn walked by as I was reviewing the announcements, and I told him about the verse Beth had shared with me to help me with my nerves. He smiled and said, "You'll be fine."

When the time came to start, I walked to the front to address the crowd. My voice wasn't shaking as I began—which was a small victory right out of the chute. My first little joke even worked, and I got people to laugh. It was going to be okay! I felt confidence seeping into my bones.

Suddenly, out of the blue, Shawn stood up and interrupted me. "Schreve," he said, "you're doing it all wrong. You haven't even greeted the visitors yet. And why are you so nervous? 'Have I not commanded you? Be strong and courageous. Do not tremble or be dismayed, for the LORD your God is with you wherever you go.'" (I couldn't believe he was using my verse against me!)

The place erupted with laughter. Nearly all the students thought Shawn's standing up to gig me was hysterical and in good fun. Everyone was laughing . . . except me. The crushing blow came when Shawn good-naturedly said, "Schreve, go sit down. I'll take over from here."

As I walked to the back of the room amid the laughter, it was all I could do not to burst into tears. My worst fears had been realized. I was embarrassed beyond belief, and my insecurity about public speaking was racing to the moon. I wanted to crawl into a hole and hide.

The smoke alarm of inferiority was blaring so loudly I couldn't hear anything else. My self-worth was on fire, and the flames were intense.

THE THING ABOUT ALARMS . . .

That humiliating morning has now been in my rearview mirror for more than a quarter century. (And by the way, Shawn apologized profusely after realizing he had hurt my feelings. He remains a dear friend to this day.) Isn't it interesting how a single, somewhat innocuous memory like that can burn with such intensity in the mind and heart for decades?

I think if we were honest, most of us would have to admit to at least minor struggles with self-doubt.

I think if we were honest, most of us would have to admit to at least minor struggles with self-doubt. Some of that is to be expected. After all, the apostle James reminded us "we all stumble in many ways" (James 3:2). But what happens when self-doubt becomes more than a passing spring shower and begins to look more like a Category 5 hurricane? What happens when those uncomfortable feelings of inferiority threaten to paralyze us and cast a shadow over everything we do and say?

That's an alarm, my friends. In fact, it's a "smoke-alarm" warning from the Lord Himself. What is the alarm telling us when feelings of embarrassment and inferiority start blaring? I believe God's message is this: *Your self-worth is on fire.*

> **EMOTIONS:** Embarrassment and insecurity
> **WARNING:** Your God-given desire for self-worth is on fire.

None of us enjoys the occasional experience of feeling like a failure, but God can use that very emotion to alert us to some deep-down, unhealthy thinking—and help us change course.

If an alarm on the ceiling alerts you to smoke in the house, the first thing you do is look for the source of that smoke. Is it upstairs, downstairs, in the kitchen, out in the garage, or from the neighbor's barbecue? Where's it coming from? In the same way, our over-the-top feelings of inferiority can alert us to serious needs in our lives, and help us trace them back to the source or root of the problem.

In fact, it can lead us right into a fresh perspective and a victorious life.

But first, we must ask ourselves, "Why am I feeling this way, and how can I turn these emotions around and let the Lord do something great through this?"

Where to Find "Worth"

John 13 allows us amazing insight into the psyche, the very core, of the Lord Jesus Christ.

Here is Someone who never felt inferior, never had self-doubt, and never questioned His own worth. There's a reason why these things are true, and John recorded it for us in his eyewitness account just hours before the Lord's arrest, trial, and crucifixion.

Now before the Feast of the Passover, Jesus knowing that His hour had come that He would depart out of this world to the Father, having loved His own who were in the world, He loved them to the end. During supper, the devil having already put into the heart of Judas Iscariot, the son of Simon, to betray Him, Jesus, knowing that the Father had given all things into His hands, and that He had come forth from God and was going back to God, got up from supper, and laid aside His garments; and taking a towel, He girded Himself.

Then He poured water into the basin, and began to wash the disciples' feet and to wipe them with the towel with which He was girded. (vv. 1–5)

In those five verses, John provided us rich insights into the mind and attitude of the Lord Jesus Christ. They are important for us to see, because Scripture commands us to "have this [same] attitude . . . which was also in Christ Jesus" (Phil. 2:5). Beyond that, God shows us how to respond when the smoke alarm goes off, indicating that our self-worth is on fire.

So, how can you turn inferiority into victory? How do you do it? Is it simply a matter of giving yourself a good pep talk? Do you look in the mirror, as Stuart Smalley used to do on *Saturday Night Live*, and say, "I'm good enough, I'm smart enough, and doggone it, people like me!"? Is that the answer for an inferiority complex?

> *How can you turn inferiority into victory? Is it simply a matter of giving yourself a good pep talk?*

No! Self-talk will only go so far. In fact, it's a little like blowing up a balloon with a hole in it: it consumes a lot of effort but provides very short-term results.

How about bragging on yourself a little in front of others? You know how it's done: Every time you see somebody, you just find a way to turn the conversation to the subject of *you*—the things you've accomplished, the places you've been, the people you know, the obstacles you've overcome. Have you ever been around people who do that—who always seem to turn every discussion back toward themselves? After a while, you begin to avoid talking to people like that, don't you? You may even find yourself going a different direction when you see them coming.

No, the answer isn't self-talk or name-dropping or boasting of your accomplishments. Neither is it getting the big job, buying the cool car, winning the big contest, or breaking some school athletic record. That's not how you get self-worth.

In fact, God tells us how to gain self-worth. There are some powerful truths that emerge from John's brief account of what happened that evening in an upstairs room as Jesus stooped down to wash the disciples' feet. If you will grasp these truths and let them really sink in and take root in your life, it will turn your debilitating inferiority into dynamic victory.

YOU HAVE INFINITE WORTH

Jesus, knowing that the Father had given all things into His hands, and that He had come forth from God . . .

JOHN 13:3

Jesus knew who He was, and where He came from. "Who am I?" wasn't a question that came to His mind or troubled Him. In His encounter with Satan in Matthew 4, the evil one tried to prod Jesus into questioning His identity. Twice he said to Jesus, *"If* You are the Son of God . . ." and then challenged Him to prove it.

"If You are the Son of God, command that these stones become bread." (v. 3)

"If You are the Son of God, throw Yourself down [from the pinnacle of the Temple]." (v. 6)

In other words, Satan wickedly yet subtly questioned, "Are You actually who You say You are? Really? Then prove it to me!"

But Jesus didn't fall into that trap. He said, in essence, *"I don't have to turn rocks into bagels or jump out of an airplane without a parachute to prove who I am. I know who I am, and I know where I've come from."*

Jesus knew He had infinite worth because He had come forth from God.

All those who have received Christ as Savior and Lord and have been born into the family of God have infinite worth as well. And when you really begin to grapple with that truth, when the incredible reality of it begins to settle into the cracks and crevices of your soul, it *will* change the way you see yourself.

All those who have received Christ as Savior and Lord and have been born into the family of God have infinite worth.

You say, "Why should I believe I have infinite worth? Isn't that just more of that shallow, glib, 'positive thinking' kind of talk?"

No, it's not. And let me give you four reasons why.

1. GOD CREATED YOU IN HIS VERY IMAGE.

God created man in His own image, in the image of God He created him; male and female He created them.

GENESIS 1:27

In Psalm 139:14, David wrote, "I will give thanks to You, for I am fearfully and wonderfully made; wonderful are Your works, and my soul knows it very well." The Hebrew term translated "wonderful" here means "distinguished," or "set apart." Picture walking into a beautiful home, and there in the entryway you see an exquisitely beautiful vase, resting on a small table. Illumined and highlighted by special lighting, it's the first thing your eyes fall upon when you enter that home, and it's obvious the homeowners want you to see and appreciate this work of art, this object of beauty, created with such great skill.

God values you. He sets you apart and wants everyone to see the skill with which you've been formed and created.

That's how God values you. He sets you apart and wants everyone to see the skill with which you've been formed and created. God designed you, formed you, and knew you while you were still taking shape in your mother's womb (see Jeremiah 1:4–5). You originated from God Himself; you're a God "original," and have been created in His very image.

In 1994, a book auctioned in New York City sold for $30.8 million. It was just a seventy-two-page notebook, containing an artist's notes and sketches. Computer magnate Bill Gates bought it, gladly laying down almost $31 million for it. Why did he pay so much for a simple sketchbook? Had he lost his mind? Were the sketches really that fabulous, the paper and cover really that expensive?

It was not because of the sketches themselves that Gates paid such a high price. Rather, it was because they were the handiwork of a man by the name of Leonardo da Vinci. Ever heard of him? Each sketch was a da Vinci original. The book, then, was valuable because of the person who created its contents.

And why are you so valuable? Why do you have such infinite worth? It's because you were personally shaped and formed by the greatest Master, God Himself. Ephesians 2:10 says this: "For we are His workmanship." You weren't made in China, and you aren't some cheap import; you are His workmanship. Imagine it standing out in bold, italic, or capital letters.

We are *His* workmanship.
We are a product of *His* design.
Our lives were conceived and designed in *His* heart.

God worked on us, fashioned us, and made us in His very image, and that makes us valuable.

2. GOD THINKS AND SPEAKS HIGHLY OF YOU.

Many of us have a negative thought track that plays over and over in our heads, morning to night. Unlike Stuart Smalley, who says, "I'm good enough, I'm smart enough, and doggone it, people like me," we look in the mirror and say just the opposite: "I'm *not* good enough. I'm *not* smart enough. I'm *not* pretty enough. And I *don't* think very many people like me."

We let that kind of polluted stream run through our minds far too often. What's the alternative? Blow up the leaking balloon with our own self-help rhetoric? No! We simply need to remember, repeat, and *believe* what God has already said about us in His Word. Gazing steadily at the truth will cause the lies and malicious slander of the adversary to melt away into the shadows. (Remember, Jesus said the devil is a liar and a thief. If the enemy can get you to believe his lies, he can steal you blind.)

What does God say about you? In Isaiah 43:4, God shares his heart and feelings with His Old Testament people, people who had rebelled against Him time and again. Yet God still thought the world of them, and He thinks the world of you too. What He says to them, He says to us today:

> *"Since you are precious in My sight,*
> *Since you are honored and I love you . . . "*

Let that sink in a minute. That's what the almighty Creator of the universe is saying to *you*. Never doubt it! He's saying, "*You're precious to Me. You're honored.*" The word translated *honor* is the Hebrew word *kabad,* literally meaning "to have weight."

The Lord is saying to you, "You're precious to Me. You're honored. I love you."

Maybe you've had the hurtful experience where someone has devalued you by belittling you or ignoring what you say, what you think, or how you feel. Perhaps someone in your family or at work has treated your words and thoughts with light regard, passing them off as if they were nothing. Maybe you've given heartfelt advice to a son or daughter, and he or she has just blown it off, paid no attention, or even laughed in your face.

Perhaps so, but God is saying here, "*You may not think you matter very much, but you matter to Me. You carry weight with Me, because I love you.*" We have value because God has given us value—and what He says goes.

In Psalm 116:1, the psalmist says, "I love the LORD, because He hears My voice and My supplications." That's a beautiful picture of the almighty God bending down low to listen to the heart cry of His child, just as a father would bend down to listen to the small voice of a little son or daughter tugging on his pant leg. That's the kind of weight God gives to our words. Why? Because we are precious to Him.

John 13:1 says, "Having loved His own who were in the world, He loved them to the end." Jesus loved His disciples to the uttermost, and that's how He loves you as well. He loves you to the end of the world and the end of the age and the end of time. What's more, He thinks highly of you.

Proverbs 23:7 says, "As he thinks within himself, so he is." What does that mean? It means you are what you think. Did you catch that? You are what you think. So what do you think when you think about yourself?

You are what you think. So what do you think when you think about yourself?

Perhaps you are like so many others who think poorly of themselves. Perhaps negative self-talk fills your mind and heart on a regular basis. Maybe you are the anti–Stuart Smalley when it comes to the subject of you. Listen, my friend: the language of your negative self-talk is *not* what God says or thinks about you! To the contrary, God thinks you're wonderful. He thinks you're special. He thinks you matter. You are a heavy hitter in His estimation. Let those wonderful thoughts sink in. God Almighty, the King of kings and Lord of lords, thinks you are terrific. Wow!

As you start thinking God's thoughts in your heart, it will change you and change the way you think about yourself.

When you consider this matter of worth—let's say, on an item that you'd like to sell—the bottom line comes to this: How much will someone pay for it?

I sold my car several years ago. It was a decked-out, fully loaded Ford Explorer, Eddie Bauer Edition. They didn't make them any nicer than the one I had. In my mind, I'd already decided it was worth sixteen thousand dollars, easy. I'd taken excellent care of that car, kept it looking sharp, and changed the oil regularly. It was in mint condition.

A man came to my house, looked the car over, and dispassionately said, "I'll give you eleven thousand for it."

I was insulted. I remember thinking, *Come on! Is there an S on my chest, for* stupid? *There is no way I'd sell that car for eleven thousand.*

When I turned down his offer, he smiled and said, "Well, that's the most I'm willing to pay."

"I can easily get more than that for this car," I told him confidently.

"Fine," he said with a nod. "But I'll check back."

Two weeks later, I still had the car . . . and I needed to sell it. It turned out that the first man had not only given me the best offer; he'd given me the *only* offer. When he came back, he brought a check for eleven thousand dollars, and I had to take it. He was the only one I found who wanted the car.

> *Worth is really determined by what someone is willing to pay. What did God pay for you and for me?*

That's the thing with worth. Worth is really determined by what someone is willing to pay. I thought my Explorer was worth sixteen thousand dollars, but in reality, it was only worth what someone would pay, in this case, eleven thousand.

What did God pay for you and for me? What was He willing to give to buy us out of the slave market of sin? First Peter 1:18–19 says, "You were not redeemed with perishable things, like silver or gold from your futile way of life inherited from your forefathers, but with precious blood as of a lamb unblemished and spotless, the blood of Christ."

That's what God paid for you and for me—*the lifeblood of His own Son.* What could be more precious, valuable, or dear than that? Silver and gold? Diamonds as big as golf balls? These things are worth *nothing*—zero—in comparison to one drop of divine blood from the innocent, sinless Lamb of God. In John 3:16 we read, "For God so loved the world [He so loved you and me], that He gave His only begotten Son." If God had given a trillion dollars for you, that would have been nothing compared to the life of His own dear Son.

Can there be a greater treasure than Jesus in all the universe? Of course not. He represents the greatest value anyone could ever conceive. And God gave that vast, incomprehensible treasure for you and for me. You were redeemed with precious blood.

So believe the truth: You have infinite worth because an infinite price was paid to redeem you, to buy you back from the slave market of sin.

Let's say that you and I were sitting on a park bench together and I took out a hundred-dollar bill and held it out to you in my hand. Can you visualize that? (If you haven't seen this bill for a while, it's the one with Benjamin Franklin on the front.) That bill is worth something in our world, right?

If I said to you, "Here's a hundred bucks; do you want it?" you would say, "Of course I do. Thanks, Jeff. You are not only handsome, but you are generous too!" (Well, maybe you wouldn't say that last part.)

But what if I first abused that hundred-dollar bill? What if I crumbled it up in a little ball? Would you still want it? I imagine you still would.

What if I stood up and stomped on it, grinding it into the dirt? Would you still take it? Would you still think it was worth having?

What if I even spit on it? Well, that wouldn't be very nice. But you could always wipe it off, and you would still have a hundred dollars. No matter what I may do to it, short of tearing it into pieces, it is still valuable and wanted.

The fact is, you may have been abused in your life—disregarded, demeaned, devalued, mistreated, ignored, sexually abused, spit upon, or stomped in the dirt. And when you think about yourself, you may be tempted to say, "I must be worthless. I'm nothing. I'm a zero."

But that is a lie! You are worth everything to God. If you had been the only person in the world, the Father would have still sent His Son for you (see Galatians 2:20). You have infinite worth. You may have truly been demeaned and disrespected by people who ought to have encouraged you and built you up. That hurts! But that is why you need to spend more and more time learning and believing what the Lord God has to say about your incredible value.

3. You possess infinite wealth.

In John 13:3, we read: "Jesus, knowing that the Father had given all things into His hands . . ." Jesus knew who He was, where He came from, and *what He had*. What did He have? Well, the verse clearly says that He had "all things." That's everything.

Do you know what you have? So many Christians really have no idea what they have. They feel that they have nothing, that the cupboards are bare and the bank accounts are empty. Yet Paul wrote to the Corinthians: "For all things belong to you, whether . . . the world or life or death or things present or things to come; all things belong to you, and you belong to Christ; and Christ belongs to God" (1 Cor. 3:21–23).

What brings an individual to the place where he or she will say terrible words like, "I don't want to live anymore"? It's because that person has become convinced that he or she has nothing: "I have no hope. I have no future. I have no opportunities. I have no prospects. I have nothing, and life isn't worth living."

Again, that is a lie from the very one who has been called "a liar and the father of lies" (John 8:44). What is the truth? If you know Jesus Christ, you have more than you could begin to imagine. You have incredible, incalculable, unfathomable wealth. Every born-again Christian is a child of the living God, a son or daughter of the King of kings and Lord of lords.

If you know Jesus Christ, you have more than you could begin to imagine. You have incredible, incalculable, unfathomable wealth.

Many years ago, I heard evangelism defined as "one beggar telling another beggar where to find bread." I understand the thought behind that expression, but in God's estimation and economy, you and I are *not* beggars. We're *not* paupers. We're *not* lower-class people living in some back alley behind a dumpster, grubbing for stale bread crumbs. If you've received Jesus Christ as Savior and Lord, you are God's own precious son or daughter. He's adopted you into His very family circle. You're a King's kid . . . and a king's kid has great wealth, especially when that king is King of the universe!

If you're His child, you enter into all His wealth. The problem we run into, however, is sheer unbelief. We can't begin to grasp or calculate what we actually possess. Second Corinthians 8:9 says this: "For you know the grace of our Lord Jesus Christ, that though He was rich, yet for your sake He became poor, that you, through His poverty, might be made rich."

Before we came to know Christ, we were truly the poorest of the poor (no matter how much money we had tucked away or what earthly toys we may have accumulated). We were "separated from the life of God" and "without hope and without God in the world" (Eph. 4:18; 2:12 NIV). You can't get any poorer than that.

But then the Lord came, died for our sins, convicted our hearts of our need for Him, and said, "Follow Me." And if we said yes to that wonderful invitation, we entered into His grace—His unmerited, undeserved favor—and actually became coheirs with Jesus Christ Himself. In Galatians, Paul wrote: "Now you are no longer a slave but God's own child. And since you are his child, *everything he has belongs to you*" (4:7 NLT; emphasis added).

In the book of Proverbs, Solomon wrote: "There is one who makes himself rich, yet has nothing; and one who makes himself poor, yet has great riches" (13:7 NKJV). I think that verse describes so many Christians. We consider ourselves poor, and yet we have great riches. *We don't realize what we have.*

When my kids were little, Disney's *The Lion King* was a smash hit movie. Debbie and the girls and I loved it. When it came out on video, we were all over it. My girls watched that movie over and over and over again. Without even trying, I became extremely familiar with almost every scene, every song, and every line of *The Lion King.*

If you know the story, you probably recall that the great lion king, Mufasa, had a little son named Simba. Simba, of course, was going to be the next king after Mufasa passed on. But little Simba had an evil uncle named Scar, who wanted to destroy Mufasa and Simba, and take the kingdom for himself. Through evil plotting and planning, Uncle Scar took Mufasa's life. And as if that weren't bad enough, he also convinced little Simba that Simba himself had caused his own father's death. As a result, he had the young lion chased out of Pride Rock. Exiled to the backside of nowhere, Simba grew up with a pig and a meerkat, living a life far below what he was created to do and be.

One day, years later, after Simba had grown, he came face-to-face with a vision of his father. Mufasa said to him in that great, booming, James Earl Jones voice, *"Simba."*

"Father?"

"Simba, you have forgotten me."

"No. How could I?"

"You have forgotten who you are, and so have forgotten me. Look inside yourself, Simba. You are more than what you have become. . . . Remember who you are. You are my son . . . . Remember who you are."[1]

I remember watching that scene (over and over) and having tears well up in my eyes, as I thought about how many Christians, myself included, so often forget who they are in Christ. So often we forget our heavenly Father; we forget that we're children of the King of all kings. As a result, we spend our time rooting around in the mud with the pigs when we ought to be running with the lions.

We live far below the level where God intended us to live. But God says to you and me, *"My child, remember who you are."*

Do you know what you have as a child of the King? In Ephesians 1:3, Paul tells us that our Father "has blessed us with every spiritual blessing in the heavenly places in Christ." Please note that it doesn't say He *will* bless us—somewhere in the sweet by-and-by—but that He *has* blessed us with these things now! You have—at this very moment—all you need to walk in victory, live a full-to-the-brim Christian life, and rise above bad circumstances.

Sometimes we say something like this: "I'm really being tested and tried at work [or at school, or at home], and I've been praying to God to give me patience." Now, we all understand what's behind a prayer like that, but the fact is, God has *already* given you patience. Or maybe you find yourself praying, "Lord, I wish You would give me more joy in my life." But why pray that? God says it's already there. It's in your bank account right now—all the joy, peace, strength, power, and discernment you need are already on deposit. He put them in your account the moment you trusted Jesus as Savior and Lord. What else could it mean when the Bible clearly says we are blessed already with *every spiritual blessing* in Christ?

But so often, we don't see, feel, understand, or believe that.

In the Schreve household, we don't write big checks for the simple reason that we don't have big money in the bank to back them up. If Debbie said, "I'd like to write a check to the church for one hundred thousand dollars," I'd have to reply, "Well, just dribble it over to the church, because it's going to bounce all over the place." We don't have that kind of money, so we don't write those kinds of checks.

Sadly, some of us tend to think the same way when it comes to spiritual things—even though the situation is vastly different. Sometimes we may feel locked up with anxiety and in great need of peace. But for some reason, we imagine that we don't have any peace at all in our spiritual bank accounts, so we can't write that check. We pray, "O God, would You please deposit some peace in my bank account, so I can get through this terrible night?"

And God says, *"My child, I've already done that. Why do you keep asking Me for things that I've already done? Why do you ask Me for gifts I've already given? Why don't you cash in on the peace that's already there?"*

The Bible says, "For no matter how many promises God has made, they are 'Yes' in Christ. And so through him the 'Amen' is spoken by us to the glory of God" (2 Cor. 1:20 NIV). In other words, when you're reading through Scripture and encounter a promise, God says, *"Yes, My son; yes, My daughter; that's for you."* It means that every time you run into a promise in the pages of God's Word, the Lord Jesus has signed that check and said, "That's in your account. It's for you." What we have to do is take that promise check and endorse it by faith by saying, "Amen," or "Yes," to God's

> *God says, "My child, why do you keep asking Me for things that I've already done? Why do you ask Me for gifts I've already given?"*

promise check. And then we cash that check at the bank of heaven. We say to God, "Father, You promised that in Christ this peace [or joy or wisdom or whatever] is already in my account. And right now I'm cashing my check to receive what You promised."

God loves it when we do that! That is walking by faith. That's saying, "Lord, I believe Your Word. And I believe You gave me this promise, just as You have given me every spiritual blessing in Christ."

Start writing checks. Start believing God.

4. YOU HAVE AN INDESCRIBABLE FUTURE.

Jesus, knowing that the Father had given all things into
His hands, and that He had come forth from God and was
going back to God . . .

JOHN 13:3

There's something about that passage that brings such peace to my heart. Not only did Jesus know who He was, where He had come from, and what He had, He also knew what was ahead. Yes, He knew very well what was *immediately* to come—betrayal, arrest, chains, humiliation, scourging . . . and finally a cross. But beyond His suffering and death, He knew what the future held for Him. *Glory!* He had come from the Father, and He was returning to the Father. He had come from heaven, and He was going back to heaven.

Every Christian needs to know what the future holds . . . and it's a glorious future for a child of the King.

Every Christian needs to know what the future holds . . . and it's a glorious future for a child of the King. God has something so great, so fabulous, so over-the-top wonderful for His own that it can't be fully fathomed or captured on paper. Every born-again believer in Jesus Christ will live for eternity— forever and ever and ever with God.

Many people have attempted to write about heaven, but their words always fall short. The apostle Paul told us they would! He said, "Things which eye has not seen and ear has not heard and which have not entered the heart of man all that God has prepared for those who love Him" (1 Cor. 2:9).

Truly, heaven is indescribable.

When R. G. Lee, the great preacher and orator of the mid-1900s, was on his deathbed, he had a vision of heaven. The message he communicated with his pastor, Dr. Adrian Rogers, was astounding. Dr. Lee said of his vision of heaven, "My vocabulary is inadequate to describe it, and I never did it justice in my preaching."[2] Though regarded by many as one of the world's greatest wordsmiths, Dr. Lee was completely unable to put the beauty and the glory of that place into words.

Years ago, I heard a true story about a little girl who stood brokenhearted at her mother's graveside. She said to the preacher who conducted the funeral service, "I know my mother's in heaven, but what is heaven like?"

The wise preacher responded sweetly and confidently, "Darling, heaven is all that the wisdom of God could conceive . . . and all that the power of God could create."

Wow. Just meditate on that awhile. How wise is God? How powerful is God? What sort of place could He create using all His wisdom and all His power? It would be a place too incredible for words. And that's exactly what heaven is.

Heaven is in my future as a believer in Jesus Christ. That's where I'm going. My name is written in the Lamb's Book of Life. It was written there in January 1980, because that was the time when I got down on my knees, cried out to God, and said, in effect, "Jesus, Son of David, have mercy on me."

And He did. He saved me and put my name in His book. And now my citizenship, as Paul said in Philippians 3:20, is in heaven.

If you know Jesus Christ, the world isn't your home—at least, not your *real* home. You're a citizen of another place, and you're just passing through this life. Your destiny is to live forever with God in heaven.

Are you struggling with inferiority? Is the smoke alarm of

embarrassment blaring in your ears? Are you questioning if you have any worth? Are you wondering, *Does anyone love me?*

Yes, Someone does. The most wonderful Someone that could ever be. He loves you with an everlasting love, and He has given you infinite worth, both *in this world and the world to come.*

TWO

LONELINESS

All by Myself

I am like a lonely owl in the desert or a restless sparrow alone on a roof.

PSALM 102:6–7 CEV

Loneliness . . . the leprosy of the West.

—MOTHER TERESA[1]

When I was ten, my parents separated. My dad moved out, got an apartment, and eventually relocated from our home state of California to some distant land called "Houston, Texas."

My parents remained separated for two and a half years, and my mom hated every day of it. Crushed by feelings of loneliness and abandonment, she cried a lot of the time. Of course, I didn't understand all that my mom was going through. All I knew was that she was really, really sad—and I had no idea how to make her happy again.

One incident stands out so clearly in my memory. We were riding in the car when a song came on the radio, the 1972 hit by Irish singer Gilbert O'Sullivan, titled, "Alone Again (Naturally)." (If you have ever heard that song, I trust you would agree with me that it is "the blues" on steroids. It expresses hopelessness unrivaled by other sad songs.)[2] I can remember my mom singing along, with tears streaming down her face.

Part of the lyrics say,

> *If [God] really does exist*
> *Why did He desert me*
> *In my hour of need?*
> *I truly am indeed,*
> *Alone again, naturally.*[3]

Ugh! Not exactly the uplifting words a person needs when she is sad and emotionally bruised already. Even so, O'Sullivan's depressing song was a Billboard Hot 100 number one single in the United States. That song obviously expressed the heart cry of many lonely and unhappy people across America.

During her separation from my dad, my mom shared with me her deepest fear. "Jeff, I'm so afraid of growing old all alone." Her words probably echo the number one fear of more people than you and I will ever know.

A LONELY PLANET

Our world is filled with lonely people. They're all around us. Every day you pass them on the street and see them looking out the window from the house next door. You brush by them on the sidewalk, catch them in your peripheral vision in the mall or at the restaurant, and maybe even offer them a quick smile in the hallways of your church.

One Christian psychiatrist called loneliness "the malady of our age." Mother Teresa, the famous nun who spent years working in the slums of Calcutta, said, "The most terrible poverty is loneliness and the feeling of being unloved."[4]

Actor Orson Welles made this despairing conclusion, "We're born alone, we live alone, we die alone. Only through our love and friendship can we create the illusion for the moment that we're not alone."[5] (No doubt that comment came from a sad, lonely man. Perhaps that explains, in part, why Welles became a chronic overeater, at one point tipping the scales at nearly four hundred pounds.)

The strange aspect to all of this, of course, is that loneliness really doesn't have much to do with your proximity to other people. You can be deeply lonely in a great crowd—even sitting in a stadium of sixty thousand people. And by the same token, you can also find yourself with a few hours of solitude and alone time and not be lonely at all.

THE TRUE DEFINITION OF LONELINESS

Loneliness, then, isn't so much a situation as an *attitude*, or state of mind. It's that sometimes overwhelming feeling that no one really knows me, cares about me, or wants me around.

A lonely person feels isolated, alienated, abandoned, and distant from others. How deeply these feelings are ingrained in our national psyche. Try doing a Google search sometime on "lonely songs" and you'll see what I mean. There are *tons* of sad, lonely, feelin'-the-blues tunes out there. And you can find them in every generation.

> *Loneliness is that sometimes overwhelming feeling that no one really knows me, cares about me, or wants me around.*

I did a quick check and was amazed by all the song titles: "All by Myself"; "Another Night Alone"; "Are You Lonesome Tonight?"; "One Is the Loneliest Number"; "Lonely Is the Night"; "Lonesome Town"; "Only the Lonely." . . . The list goes on and on.

In 1966, Paul McCartney wrote the Beatles hit song, "Eleanor Rigby," about a lonely old woman who "picks up the rice in the church where a wedding has been." Paul based the song on memories he had as a boy, when he would visit with elderly people and try to help them. In a magazine interview a few years ago, he said, "When I was a kid I was very lucky to have a real cool dad, a working-class gent, who always encouraged us to give up our seat on the bus for old people.

"This led me into going round to pensioners' houses. It sounds a bit goody-goody, so I don't normally tell too many people. There were a couple of old ladies and I used to go round and say, 'Do you need any shopping done?' These lonely old ladies were something I knew about growing up, and that was what 'Eleanor Rigby' was about—the fact that she died and nobody really noticed. I knew this went on."[6]

Wasn't it Elvis who sang, "I'm so lonesome I could cry"? Elvis knew about loneliness.

So did David.

Although Israel's greatest king reigned for forty years, surrounded by advisers, warriors, and family, in his early days he spent a great deal of time alone. First, it was as a shepherd in the wilderness, keeping watch over his dad's sheep. In later years, he was on the run from the insanely jealous King Saul (Psycho Saul, as I like to call him), hiding out in caves, canyons, deserts, and lonely, forsaken hideouts in the wilderness.

David summed up loneliness in Psalm 142, written, appropriately enough, from the black depths of a limestone cave.

> *I cry aloud with my voice to the LORD;*
> *I make supplication with my voice to the LORD.*
> *I pour out my complaint before Him;*
> *I declare my trouble before Him.*
> *When my spirit was overwhelmed within me,*
> *You knew my path. . . .*
> *Look to the right and see;*

For there is no one who regards me;
There is no escape for me;
No one cares for my soul. (vv. 1–4)

Wow! That is loneliness personified. A few lines later, David wrote: "Give heed to my cry, for I am brought very low" (v. 6).

Brought very low. If you have ever experienced the pangs of loneliness—perhaps after a broken engagement, a spouse's betrayal, or the loss of a loved one—you know exactly what David meant by those three words.

WHAT IS THE MESSAGE IN LONELINESS?

EMOTION: Loneliness
WARNING: Your God-given desire for companionship is on fire.

God's message in the emotion of loneliness is, "Pay attention to this: Your God-given desire for companionship has been thwarted. Your built-in longing for relationships is being short-circuited."

God is a personal God, a relational God, and when He created us in His own image, He built into us the desire for companionship and a yearning for authentic relationships. As we review the creation account in the book of Genesis, we find that, though God was very pleased with His creation and said five times in chapter 1 that "it was good," He added these shocking words in chapter 2: "It is not good for the man to be alone" (v. 18). Not good? No. Not good at all, because God made us for relationships—plural. We are to have a relationship with Him *and* relationships with others.

NOT GOD'S PLAN

God doesn't want anyone to live a lonely life. That is why the Bible says in Psalm 68:6 that "God makes a home for the lonely." He has a special love and care for those who are suffering the pains of loneliness.

Even so, even as you're reading these words, you may be saying, "But, Jeff, I'm just overwhelmed with loneliness. I am so lonely I have trouble getting out of bed in the morning. I can't think of anyone who really cares about me. I feel like David in the recesses of the dark, lonely cave."

Regardless of how lonely you may be feeling right now, one thing is for certain: God doesn't want you to live a lonely life.

Regardless of how lonely you may be feeling right now, one thing is for certain: God doesn't want you to live a lonely life. In fact, He wants to speak to your heart today, right from the pages of this chapter, and turn that miserable loneliness of yours around. He wants to help you discover victorious living and learn where to turn and what to do when you're feeling so isolated and alone.

The wonderful thing about knowing Jesus as Savior and Lord is that in Him we have One who can relate to our loneliness. He has experienced all of the same human emotions that you and I have. The book of Hebrews assures us, "We do not have a high priest who cannot sympathize with our weaknesses, but One who has been tempted in all things as we are, yet without sin. Therefore let us draw near with confidence to the throne of grace, so that we may receive mercy and find grace to help in time of need" (4:15–16). We can bring our loneliness to Jesus and know for certain that He understands—on a deeply personal, experiential level. Like

His human ancestor David, He, too, was "brought very low" in His life on earth, and He can personally identify with that awful, empty ache in the soul that goes deeper than words can express.

But Jesus doesn't just leave us in our sorrow and heaviness of heart. He offers us a way out.

In His Sermon on the Mount, Jesus gave us insight into the way life really works—and the secret for emerging from those sometimes overwhelming feelings of loneliness and isolation. In Luke 6, after startling His audience with an exhortation to "love your enemies," Jesus capped off His point with this surprising word picture in verse 38: "Give, and it will be given to you. They will pour into your lap a good measure—pressed down, shaken together, and running over. For by your standard of measure it will be measured to you in return."

On the issue of loneliness, I'd like to zero in on one key word in that extraordinary statement: *give.* And I want to share with you three simple encouragements concerning that word—encouragements with the power to transform your loneliness into blessing and lasting benefit if you will put them into practice in your life.

1. When you feel lonely, give yourself to the Lord.

A lonely person feels as if nobody cares, and that he or she is without a true friend in the world. When the loneliness alarm goes off in your own soul and says, "There's no relationship in my life," it's time to find yourself a friend.

Proverbs 18:24 tells us, "A man of too many friends comes to ruin, but there is a friend who sticks closer than a brother." That Friend's name is Jesus.

Do you associate the word "friend" with God? So many people I know would simply never do that. They see God as Lord, as King, as Almighty, as Creator, as seated on a rainbow-wrapped throne in the middle of a lightning bolt, somewhere in an incomprehensible place called heaven. And He truly is an awesome and majestic King.

But how do you *get close* to the King of everything? How can you and I possibly approach the Sovereign of the universe, described in Hebrews 12:29 as "a consuming fire"?

Consider this: God is also revealed in Scripture as Father. That designation would break down some walls for some of us, and we might say, "Okay, well, that makes God seem a little less distant. I can get close to a Father."

But what if you had a terrible father? What if your father was abusive, or an alcoholic, or painfully absent from your life? What if your father beat you, demeaned you, or sexually abused you? Perhaps you say, "Man, when I think of God as Father, it makes me want to run the other direction."

> God says, "I want you to start thinking about Me as a friend . . . because I'm a friend who sticks closer than a brother."

So people run from the King of the universe because they've never known a king, can't relate to a king, and couldn't feel close to a king. Or they back away from a Father in heaven because their earthly fathers were cruel, uncaring, unpredictable, or unfaithful.

But God is also presented in Scripture as a *friend*.

We've all had some friends in our lives, even if it was years ago. We know about friends. A friend is someone who actually likes us, wants to be with us, appreciates our companionship, and looks forward to seeing us. And God says, *"I want you to start thinking about Me as a friend . . . because I'm a friend who sticks closer than a brother."*

TALKING TO MY FRIEND

Some time ago, I found myself really struggling with a particular issue. It was a failing in my life that disappointed and grieved me, and I just needed someone to talk to. But I thought to myself, *Who can I talk to about this?* It's not easy for pastors to talk about areas of struggle in their lives with members of their church family. After all, a pastor is supposed to "have it all together." Right?

I knew I should go to God, but when I thought of Him as the great King on that heavenly throne, I found myself shying away. *I can't talk to Him about something like this. He's not going to like what I'm struggling with.* I could go to Him as my heavenly Father, but again, I felt reluctant. This wasn't something you'd easily talk about with your dad, even the best dad.

What I needed was a friend. And in that moment the Lord spoke to my heart. He said, *"Jeff, I'm a Friend. You can talk to Me. I'm a Friend who sticks closer than a brother. I'm a Friend of sinners. Are you struggling with sin, Jeff? Talk to Me about it. I'm not your condemner; I'm your Wonderful Counselor and Friend."*

In fact, Hebrews 13 also tells us clearly that "the LORD is my helper" (v. 6). On some level, most of us probably believe that. And yet some of us feel reluctant or afraid to go to God with our problems, our real-life struggles, and the ache of our loneliness. Why? Because we somehow think He won't understand, He won't really care, or maybe He'll just lose patience with us because we keep struggling with the same dumb things, time and again.

But that's not true. The Lord says, *"I am a Friend—a true and loyal Friend. Talk to Me. Share your heart with Me."* God *wants* us to do that.

When you think about it, how else do you get to be best friends with anyone? It isn't by holding yourself aloof and making small talk. No, it's by sharing your heart. Best friends share heart stuff, deep stuff.

DAVID

David was called a man after God's own heart (see Acts 13:22). Yet, he certainly had his share of difficulties, failures, and tragedies in life. As we've noted, he experienced years as a fugitive, running from one backcountry hideout to the next. But through all those years and all that loneliness, he really never lost the sense that God was there with him. Scripture portrays David as someone who had learned to encourage and strengthen himself in the Lord, even in the darkest, loneliest, and most hopeless of times (see 1 Samuel 30:6).

One of the keys to David's greatness was that he learned to share his heart with God. In Psalm 62:8, David wrote: "Trust in Him at all times, O people; pour out your heart before Him. God is a refuge for us. Selah." That last word, *Selah*, means "Pause and let that sink in."[7] God is a refuge for us. In other words, He is a safe place. You can share your heart of hearts with Him.

> *God is a refuge for us. In other words, He is a safe place. You can share your heart of hearts with Him.*

What is on your heart today? What kind of hurt are you carrying? What sort of difficulty are you wrestling with? What wounds are you hiding, deep down where no one else can see? The Lord says, *"Come to Me. Pour that out to Me. Share all of it with Me. Don't hold it inside. Let Me be your best Friend in the midst of your suffering, turmoil, and loneliness."*

HE WILL NEVER FORSAKE YOU

But maybe you feel that God just really *can't* relate to you. "There's no way He could know what it's like to be me," you say, "what it feels like to be left out, to be so alone, to be ostracized." Is that so? Scripture says of Jesus that He was "forsaken of men, a man of sorrows, and acquainted with grief" (Isa. 53:3). He knows what it's like to be abandoned.

When the mob arrested Him in the Garden, *everyone* hightailed it and left Him alone. Even James. Even John. But what about Peter? In the house of Caiaphas, at the very moment when Jesus most needed a friend to stand up for Him, Peter, the one who had boasted that he was ready to go with Him to prison and even to death, loudly and profanely denied three times that he even knew Him.

Talk about feeling alone! But at least Jesus had His Father, right? Yes . . . but then, on the cross, we hear Him cry out, "My God, My God, why have *You* forsaken Me?" (Mark 15:34; emphasis added). In the darkest, loneliest, most hellish moment of horror and agony, God the Father turned His back on Jesus. As Jesus took upon Himself all of our sin on the cross—the sin of all the world for all time and the punishment that rightfully belongs to *us*—God, the righteous and holy Judge, stepped away from His own dear Son, and left Him to suffer and die—alone.

For our sakes, He *had* to.

God deserted Jesus so that you and I would never have to be deserted, so we would never have to be forsaken. Jesus had to be alone . . . so that you and I

In Hebrews 13:5, in the original Greek, the Lord says, "I will not, never, never leave you; I will not, never forsake you." He wants you to know that you can count on Him to be there for you.

would never have to be alone. Not today. Not tomorrow. Not a million years from now.

In Hebrews 13:5, the Lord says, "I will never desert you, nor will I ever forsake you." In the original Greek, this passage literally reads, "I will not, never, never leave you; I will not, never forsake you."[8] There are five negatives in one sentence. That makes for poor grammar but great theology! I trust you get the point: *He will never abandon you.*

It's been said that a friend is one who walks in when the whole world has walked out. God is that sort of friend. He will stand with you, at your side, when everyone else has made their excuses and faded away. That was Paul's testimony. During his final imprisonment in Rome, in one of the last sentences he ever penned, he wrote, "At my first defense, no one came to my support, but everyone deserted me. . . . But the Lord stood at my side and gave me strength" (2 Tim. 4:16–17 NIV).

If you know Christ, you can know for certain that He'll stand at your side too. When you're in the dark cave, and it seems as if the whole world is against you and no one cares for your soul, the Lord is there to say, *"I care. Come to Me. Rest in Me. Give Me your heart."*

That's my first encouragement. When you're feeling lonely, give yourself to the Lord. It's the best, wisest, and most wonderful thing you could ever do.

2. WHEN YOU FEEL LONELY, GIVE YOURSELF TO OTHERS.

Luke 6 talks a lot about love. In fact, it talks about the highest kind of love, God's kind of love, a love so unique that the Greek language had to coin a new word for it: *agape.*

This kind of love is not based on conditions or on doing certain things or behaving in a certain way. *Agape* love doesn't say, "If you do this and this and this, then I'll love you." It says, "I love you *in spite of* what you do. I just love you because I choose to love you. If you strike Me on one cheek, I'll offer you the other. If you hate Me, curse Me, and mistreat Me, I'll still love you, bless you, and pray for you." That is God's *agape* love for you and me . . . and what He commands us to have for others.

Now, how in the world does anybody love like that? To say, "It's tough to do" is a gross understatement.

Do you have people in your life who just don't like you? Maybe even hate you? How are you supposed to show *agape* to them?

Sadly enough, I have some people like that in my life. They just don't like me at all . . . and they let me know it by their actions and words. I have to honestly ask myself, could I really bless the one who would suddenly turn on me and punch me out? Would I willingly offer him the other cheek for more of the same? More likely, if left to my natural inclinations, I would offer him the other *fist*.

That's what we do, isn't it? If someone pokes us, we poke back. If someone slaps us on the face, we return the favor. But the Lord is saying, *"Don't do it that way. I want you to give love to other people, even when they don't deserve it."* Giving love to others goes a long way in removing loneliness from you.

Perhaps you say, "Well, that's just not in me to do that."

No, maybe not. But it's in *Him*. It's in God. And that's what His *agape* love is all about. When you receive Christ as Savior and Lord, the Holy Spirit of God comes into your heart, and the Lord begins to nudge you to let Him love people *through* you. It's not your love; it's *His* love that flows through you like water through a hose.

OUR PURPOSE

When we're lonely, we lose sight of our very purpose for being here: to be a channel of His love! God wants us to give ourselves

God wants to love people into His kingdom through you and me.

to Him so that He can give Himself to us. As He does, the overflow of His unfathomable love just naturally spills over and splashes on the hearts of other thirsty people. God wants to love people into His kingdom through you and me. What an awesome thought to really ponder.

GUSHING LOVE

The Lord loves anybody and everybody with whom you come in contact. And the fact is, He has given you an endless reservoir of love for the men, women, and children in your life—if you'll just open the floodgates and allow that love to come surging over the spillway. The book of Romans tells us that "the love of God has been poured out within our hearts through the Holy Spirit who was given to us" (5:5). That English word *pour* might be a little too mild of a translation. In the literal Greek, the word means "to gush, spill, or to be shed abroad."[9]

In other words, it's not a trickle of love; it's a fast-running stream, overflowing its banks.

God says, *"I have gushed out my agape love into your heart, and I want to love other people through you."* You see, that's your job and my job. We're ambassadors for Christ. We are called to be channels of His love. It's the perfect cure for loneliness.

Yet, as I said earlier, when we get lonely, too often we lose sight of this principal calling on earth. As a result, we become self-centered and self-focused. All of us, of course, think about ourselves and our own needs from time to time. That's just human nature. For the lonely person, however, self becomes an all-consuming priority. The Lord never wants us to be consumed and preoccupied with self. He wants us to be consumed with Christ and think about touching others with His love.

When you boil it down, *loneliness is closely linked to self-pity.* What words are always recycling through the mind of a chronically lonely individual? "Nobody ever calls *me*. Nobody ever comes to see *me*. Nobody ever befriends *me*. Nobody cares for *me*." Me, me, me, me.

But even in those Linda Ronstadt, "poor-poor-pitiful-me" moments, if we're really listening, we can hear the Holy Spirit say, *"Hey, wait a minute. You're just focused way too much on* you."[10] Philippians 2:3 says, "Do nothing from selfishness . . . but . . . let each of you regard one another as more important than himself."

Even in those Linda Ronstadt, "poor-poor-pitiful-me" moments, if we're listening, we can hear the Holy Spirit say, "Hey, wait a minute. You're just focused way too much on you."

No matter how tough you have it, no matter how lonely you might be, the Lord says, "Regard one another as more important than yourself." It's really a matter of lifting up your eyes and elevating your field of vision a little. The Lord would sometimes say words like that to His disciples: "Lift up your eyes, and look" (John 4:35 KJV). And if you do that, chances are you'll see someone else—a hurting man, woman, or child out there who has it worse than you do and desperately needs to experience the touch of a loving God.

I heard a true story about an elderly lady, a shut-in, who had lost her husband, had no family, and spent most of her time alone. She couldn't get out, could no longer make it to church, and began to feel overwhelmed with loneliness.

One day she prayed, "Lord, I'm so lonely, and no one ever calls or comes to see me. I'm out of the flow of church, so people don't really know me anymore or even remember me. It's just so devastating, Lord, to live out my life this way."

But she went on to say, "God, I know You're not done with me yet. If You were done with me, then I know You would call me home. And so, Lord, I know You still have something for me to do."

After getting up from her knees, she felt as though the Lord had impressed her to pray for people in her church, and to write a few notes of encouragement. Obedient to the Lord's voice, she pulled out her church pictorial directory and began to thumb through it, looking at the faces on each page, and praying for individuals and families. Later, she began to write little notes of encouragement and mail them to those people.

Not long after this, something amazing happened: she started to get notes *back*. Her phone began to ring. People began dropping in on her for visits. She had never asked or even hinted for any of that. She never told anyone about her feelings of isolation. she simply began to take an interest in other people, and let the Lord love them through her. And as she did, her loneliness melted away as love came back to her in a hundred different ways.

If you find yourself in a trough of loneliness, I'm not saying that this will be an easy thing for you to start. The first moves out of a deep pit are always the most difficult. The fact is, if you're lonely and brokenhearted, you won't *feel* like giving yourself to God, let alone giving love to others. How do you give when you have nothing? How do you pour out when your cup is empty?

That brings us to the most astonishing part of God's whole plan.

3. WHEN YOU FEEL LONELY, UNDERSTAND GOD'S LAW OF GIVING.

Look again at Luke 6:38: "Give, and it will be given to you. They will pour into your lap a good measure—pressed down, shaken together, and running over."

What is the Lord's plan of giving to you when you are lonely?

He gives to you *when you give to* others. This is the basic principle of sowing and reaping that appears over and over in the Scriptures. You reap what you sow. In fact, you reap *more* than you sow.

So maybe today as you're reading this book, you're saying, "Jeff, when I look out at the field of my life, it's pretty barren. I have some acquaintances, but no real friends. The alarm of loneliness is going off in my soul because I don't have any relationships."

God might reply, "*Well, what have you been sowing? You reap what you sow. You harvest what you plant. If you don't have friends, then start sowing seeds of friendship.*"

That's what the elderly shut-in did. She, too, felt empty and desolate. But as she began to sow tiny seeds of friendship, it wasn't long before she began to experience a harvest of new friends and an end to her constant loneliness.

God responds to your giving by giving to you.

God responds to your giving by giving to you. As Proverbs 18:24 says, "A man who has friends must himself be friendly" (NKJV). So start sowing seeds of love, friendship, concern, and encouragement, and see how long loneliness remains an issue.

Beware of the Social Vampire Syndrome

I mentioned before what can happen to a lonely person who is not careful. He or she can easily become *self*-absorbed, *self*-centered, *self*-focused. Unfortunately, if that lonely, self-focused individual doesn't begin to move into God's plan of giving and receiving, sowing and reaping, he or she may soon slip into what I like to call the "social vampire syndrome."

A social vampire is a person who is "all about me." He is so focused on self and so desperate for attention that if anyone shows him the slightest bit of interest, he will latch on to that person like a vampire, and begin to suck the life out of him.

Let's say you're just passing someone in the hallway at work or at school, and as you're going by, you smile and say, "Hi. How are you doing?" What you're expecting is a greeting, a returned smile, and maybe a two- or three-word answer.

What you don't want is the person's life story. Not right there. Not right then. "How are you doing?" is just a polite salutation, not an invitation for a marathon counseling session. But ask a social vampire that innocent little question and he'll buttonhole you right there and tell you, in great and painful detail, everything you don't want to know. All his trials. All his troubles. All his aches and pains. I remember Dr. Adrian Rogers once saying, "There are some people that I never ask how they're doing . . . because they'll *tell* me." He didn't have the time or emotional energy for their marathon answer.

Friendship is all about sowing into someone else's life, not holding them captive to your loneliness.

Some of these same people wonder, *Why doesn't anyone call me? Why won't anyone listen to me? Why don't people want to be with me?* It's because people generally avoid someone who clings to them, corners them, monopolizes their time, and sucks the life out of them. To no one's great surprise, social vampires don't have friends. A true friend is a giver, not a taker. Friendship is all about sowing into someone else's life, not holding them captive to your loneliness.

44

Helping a Social Vampire

My friend, mentor, and seminary professor Dr. Wayne McDill is what you might call a straight shooter. And where Scripture talks about "speaking the truth in love," Dr. McDill is always working on the love side of that equation. Why? Because he has the truth part down cold! I love this guy, and part of what I love about him is that he will always tell you the truth, and you'll always know exactly where you stand with him.

One day in preaching class, Dr. McDill told the story about a student in seminary who had some of those social vampire tendencies. This young man always went around looking forlorn, moping, and muttering to himself, "No one likes me. Nobody ever calls me. Life is terrible."

In time, this student went to see Dr. McDill for comfort, sympathy, and a "There, there, you poor dear." Was he in for a rude awakening.

After listening to the whining for a few minutes, Dr. McDill said, "Why are you telling me this stuff? Do I look like your mother?" When the young man looked up, stunned and surprised, the wise professor went on. "You say you don't have any friends? Well, *look* at you! Who would want to be your friend? You're not friendly. You never smile. You never show any interest in others. You mope around all the time. You dress sloppy—look at that shirt! It's all crumpled and dirty. Besides that, you need a shave."

McDill wasn't finished. "Do you know what you need to do? You need to go out and buy a new shirt, a new pair of slacks, get reacquainted with your razor, and start combing your hair. And if you want to have friends, start sowing seeds of friendship. Quit focusing on yourself, and start opening your eyes to the needs of other people. *You* become the person who looks for lonely people to befriend them. Don't wait for somebody to befriend you. You befriend them."

After Dr. McDill related this story to the class, he said, "Do you know what that guy did then? He took his car and drove to the mall. He bought some better-looking clothes, began to shave and clean himself up . . . and he started sowing seeds of friendship everywhere he could. He began to find out about people, learn their names, and let them know he cared about them.

"And the strangest thing happened," Dr. McDill went on. "His phone began to ring. People began to speak to him and hang with him, and even seek him out. He had friends to do things with, and life wasn't lonely anymore. There was a transformation!"

IT'S ALL ABOUT GIVING

I can't help but think of the story of the sweet lady named Dorcas in Acts 9. The text says of her: "She was always doing kind things for others and helping the poor" (v. 36 NLT).

When Dorcas became ill and died, her distraught friends quickly sent word to the apostle Peter, asking him to come and raise her from the dead. When Peter came into the room where they had laid her, "all the widows stood beside him, weeping and showing all the tunics and garments that Dorcas used to make while she was with them" (v. 39).

If you know the story, you know that it had a happy ending. But what impresses me is that this woman—probably single and alone— had so endeared herself to her community with acts of kindness and care *that they simply refused to let her go*!

Dorcas shows us the way out of loneliness. Instead of hiding behind walls, you break through them. You change the paradigm. You *give.* God responds to your giving by giving to you—and by giving much, much more than you did.

Give a cupful, and God says, *"I'll give you a gallon."*

Give a gallon, and God says, *"I'll give you a barrelful."*

Give a barrelful, and God says, *"I'll give you a truckload."*

You can never, ever out-give God. Never!

How many friends do you want? You'll determine the amount you get by what you invest, by what you give. Scripture says, "He who sows sparingly shall also reap sparingly, but he who sows bountifully shall also reap bountifully" (2 Cor. 9:6). So if you want a big crop—a large group of friends who will care about you—then care about them! And don't just care about one or two; care about a lot of people.

> *Dorcas shows us the way out of loneliness. Instead of hiding behind walls, you break through them. You change the paradigm. You give.*

- Write (brief) notes and e-mails to them.
- Encourage them when they're sad or grieving.
- Celebrate with them when they do something well.
- Refuse to criticize or judge them in your heart, but rather express your concern for them and pray for them.

In short, just love people. And you will be loved in return.

SKIP'S STORY

I have a good friend named Skip Oliver, a police officer in Houston. When Skip was just seven, he and his father were in a terrible car wreck. His dad, who was a diabetic, had forgotten to take his insulin that day, and passed out at the wheel. The car slammed into a ditch, and little Skip, who wasn't wearing a seat belt, was hurled straight through the windshield.

Skip's face was deeply cut—literally ripped open—by the glass, with shards of it even penetrating his throat. He had to endure more than 250 stitches in his face alone.

Even after three intensive plastic surgeries, Skip's face was disfigured for life. He could never smile correctly after that because so many facial nerve endings had been severed.

Children, of course, can be merciless to anyone who is a little "different," and Skip was *a lot* different. Because his face was distorted and he couldn't smile right, he had to endure the taunts and the laughter almost every day of his life.

"I hated to have my picture taken," Skip told me, "because of the way I looked, and the way I couldn't smile." As a result of all the verbal abuse, he began to shy away from people, which made him feel more and more isolated and alone as the years went by.

Skip, however, had one huge blessing in his life: a godly mom who loved the Lord and loved her boy, praying for him and encouraging him every day. Gradually, Skip began to overcome his instinctive tendency to hide from people and draw away from them, and started sowing seeds of kindness and friendship instead.

I became acquainted with Skip when I was on staff at Champion Forest Baptist Church in Houston, preaching on Wednesday nights. The first time I ever met him, he came up to me after the service and said, "Hey, I really like the way you preach."

I thanked him, and then he said, "In your sermons, you sometimes talk about the Houston Rockets. Do you follow the Rockets?"

"I love the Rockets," I told him.

"Do you like Hakeem Olajuwon?" (A big superstar for the Rockets at that time.)

"Yes! He's my favorite player," I said.

"He's one of my best friends," Skip said. "Would you like to meet him?"

I said, "Yes, I'd like to meet him." But I was thinking to myself, *Oh yeah, sure. Hakeem Olajuwon is one of your best friends. Right.*

Two weeks later I found myself, with Skip, in Hakeem's living room! He was indeed Skip's close friend, and because of Skip, I got to spend forty-five minutes with this great sports star. It was amazing!

As I began to get to know Skip better, it seemed to me as though he knew everyone. He had more friends than anyone I had ever known.

About ten years ago, I picked up the phone and called Skip, just to see how he was doing.

"Hi, Jeff," he said. "I can't talk right now. I'm on the golf course."

"Oh yeah? Who are you playing golf with?"

"Michael Jordan."

"My soul!" I said. "How do you get to play golf with Michael Jordan?"

"Well, I got invited."

"Who invited you?"

"Clyde Drexler." (Another NBA legend.)

Somehow, Skip ended up being buddies with all kinds of famous people. Around Houston, at least, there seemed to be very few people who didn't know and love Skip Oliver.

Do you know what made the difference? Do you know why Skip

had so many friends? It's because he was constantly investing in people's lives. Every time Skip called me, he would say, "Jeff, is there anything you need? Is there anything I can do for you?"

And it wasn't just words. He meant it! I knew that if I were ever in need, I could count on Skip to help me.

Before a sermon I preached in which I shared Skip's story, I called him to verify all the information and ask him about his celebrity friends. (Note: Skip has lots of friends, some of which just happen to be celebrities.) He said, "Yes, I am friends with a lot of these famous athletes. But do you know why? It's because they're always being "hit up" by people who want to take from them, who want money from them, who want this or that from them. But I never want anything from them. I just want to give to them.

"Besides," he added, "I'm not impressed with their celebrity status. You know what impresses me? Guys like you, who preach the gospel."

Who wouldn't love Skip?

The fact is, we can follow his example. And like him, we don't have to be lonely anymore.

WILL YOU DO IT?

Do you want to silence the smoke alarm of loneliness? You can start by giving your heart to the Lord, by letting Jesus become your best friend. And then, in faith—even if you don't feel anything at first—you can begin to give to others, sowing seeds of friendship and kindness in their lives.

Now, don't give to get. Don't give with getting as your motive, because then you will be consumed with self and the "it's all about me" paradigm all over again. That kind of giving doesn't receive a blessing. As one Christian philanthropist astutely remarked, "If you give because it pays, it won't pay." No, just give, expecting nothing in return . . . and God will give back to you. He sees it all, and He rewards those who do things His way.

THREE

FRUSTRATION

A Real Nowhere Man

"Before I formed you in the womb I knew you, and before you were born I consecrated you."

JEREMIAH 1:5

When Debbie and I first got married, I naturally assumed I would be responsible for fixing things around the house. She did too.

It's a reasonable assumption, isn't it?

I grew up in a family where my dad fixed broken stuff, built things when he had to, and generally kept the household machinery up and running. Debbie's dad did the same thing. That's what guys do, right?

It's true I'd never paid much attention to learning how to accomplish those home repair tasks as I was growing up, but I somehow believed that when the need arose in my own home, the knowledge would "just be there."

Funny thing, it wasn't. And maybe it wasn't so funny after all because this has been a real weakness in my life. Try as I might, I've never been very good at fixing things. I often joke that when I was young, I had a mechanical bypass. If it is something more complicated than changing a lightbulb, invariably I'm going to have trouble.

It's not that Debbie hasn't been encouraging. One Christmas she even bought me a nice, shiny set of new tools, including an electric drill—the symbol of true manhood. All real men *must* have an electric drill, she thought. So now I had one . . . but, alas, it didn't transform me into "Mr. Fix-it."

I'll never forget the day when Debbie asked me to put in a doggie door for our little dog, Maggie. She had picked up the do-it-yourself kit at the hardware store, brought it home, and set it down in front of me. It came in a big box that read, "easy installation."

I liked that part.

When I pulled out the directions, however, right off the bat it read, "Take your electric drill . . ." *What?* That's "easy installation"? To me, easy installation starts off with "Grab your hammer . . ." But right away, the doggie-door instructions were asking me to employ a power tool. It was already getting intimidating.

I got out my measuring tape, made the appropriate marks on the lower part of our door, selected (what I hoped was) the appropriate drill bit, lay down on my stomach, and began drilling. And drilling and drilling and drilling. But nothing happened.

As the sweat began to pour, the frustration I had so wanted to keep at bay began to boil up inside me. I thought, *This is going to take forever. I can't get even one hole through this stupid door.*

It didn't help at all when Debbie came into the room and started laughing. I realized it was just a nervous laugh, and she didn't mean anything by it, but a laughing wife and a frustrated husband don't make for a happy day.

"Debbie," I said frustratedly from my uncomfortable, perspiration-filled position on the floor, "at this rate this is going to take me ten or twelve hours. I may very well lose my salvation over this doggie door . . . and I don't even like the dog! Is it really worth it?"

"No," she said quickly. "No, it's not worth it. Let's call Gene."

Gene lived down the street and was one of those guys who can do almost anything with his own two hands. So Gene cheerfully responded to our call and drove up to the house in his pickup. As he walked up to the door, I couldn't help noticing that he had sawhorses in the back of his truck. What kind of guy drives around with sawhorses?

Gene did. It was as if Bob Vila had come over to save the day!

After quickly studying the situation, Gene had two immediate suggestions. First, he informed me that we had a *metal* door, which required a certain type of drill bit. (Metal? For crying out loud, who has a metal door?) And then he suggested that we take the door off its hinges. What an idea! I wished I'd thought of it, instead of trying to drill my way through a metal door, lying on my stomach.

In a heartbeat, Gene popped the door off the hinges and placed it on his ever-present sawhorses that he carried in the back of his truck. And power tools? He seemed to have more selection than Home Depot. In twenty effortless minutes, he had the doggie door in and my door back on. It was a task that would have taken me hours and hours and eaten me alive with frustration.

God bless Gene. The Lord has gifted him with handyman skills I can only dream about. The long and short of it was this: I was trying to do a job I wasn't really equipped to do, and in the process, I was becoming very, very frustrated.

An Unhappy Combination

Frustration is something of a combination emotion—an unhappy blend of anger and discouragement. You're angry because you've been kept from your goal, and you're discouraged because your efforts didn't bring you success.

Everyone gets frustrated from time to time. You're trying to fix the car, but somehow you've made it worse, rather than better. You get frustrated with your computer because you're trying to save something, and the program freezes up right in the middle of the process, sending your document into the Twilight Zone. Or maybe you're frustrated with school because you can't figure out the homework, and the instructions seem to make no sense at all. It makes you a little angry, and then a little discouraged. Or maybe it makes you *a lot* angry, and *very* discouraged.

Frustration is something of a combination emotion—an unhappy blend of anger and discouragement. You're angry because you've been kept from your goal, and you're discouraged because your efforts didn't bring you success.

There's nothing unusual about flare-ups of frustration from time to time. Frustrations come with the territory for imperfect people living in a sin-warped world. Some people, however, aren't just frustrated with this setback or that difficulty; they're frustrated with *life*. Could that be true of you?

Maybe things aren't good at home with your marriage or family. Perhaps you find yourself chronically unemployed, or in a boring, dead-end job and can't seem to get ahead. It's just the same-old, same-old. Or possibly you're caught in some destructive addiction that, try as you might, you just can't seem to break. It is normal and natural for us to get frustrated when we feel as though we're just treading water, working hard but *going* nowhere. And we begin to ask ourselves, "What am I here for, anyway?" We live for the weekend, but then when the weekend comes, nothing seems to work out. Ugh.

Nowhere Man Is Frustrated

Back in 1965, the Beatles released a song that people have sung for decades. Do you remember "Nowhere Man"?

He's a real nowhere man
Sitting in his Nowhere Land
Making all his nowhere plans for nobody
Doesn't have a point of view
Knows not where he's going to
Isn't he a bit like you and me?[1]

In a 1971 interview with *Rolling Stone* magazine, John Lennon admitted that the whole song grew out of a time of frustration in his life. He had been trying to write a song for an album, but couldn't come up with anything. He said, "I thought of myself sitting there, doing nothing, and getting nowhere. . . . So I just lay down and tried to not write and then this came out. The whole thing in one gulp."[2]

If you're living like a nowhere man, a nowhere woman, in a nowhere land, you're going to be frustrated. The God who created you in His image is a God of meaning and purpose. And if you don't live your life with a sense of meaning, purpose, and fulfillment, frustration will come and fill you with misery.

EMOTION: Frustration
WARNING: Your God-given desire for meaning and purpose
     is on fire.

ARE YOU HEARING THE SMOKE ALARM?

If you don't do anything in response to the smoke alarm of frustration, the fire will either break out in a big explosion, hurting both yourself and those you love, or it will just burn you away from the inside, leaving you bored and apathetic toward life.

Do you know what *apathy* means? It comes from a Greek word that literally means "no feeling" or "without passion." People who become apathetic have an attitude that says, "Who cares? What does it matter? I have a crummy life, and nothing really means anything. I just live for the weekend because that's the only time I can ever have any fun. All I do during the week really doesn't make any difference at all."

That, my friend, is a living death.

To say "no passion" is very close to saying "no life," and that is not what God intends for you. He didn't create you to live a meaningless existence, seared on the inside by the smoldering flames of frustration.

In fact, the very frustration you feel is there to alert you to the fact that something has gone wrong in your soul, and it's time to check in with your Creator. God wants you to deal with that frustration before it burns out all the joy and happiness and peace in your life. He wants to speak to your heart about meaning and purpose.

"Before I Formed You . . . I Knew You"

When the young Jewish priest Jeremiah received his commission from the Lord to be a prophet, he really struggled with the whole idea. Later in life, however, the Lord's words must have been a comfort to him:

> Now the word of the LORD came to me saying, "Before I formed you in the womb I knew you, and before you were born I

consecrated you; I have appointed you a prophet to the nations." Then I said, "Alas, Lord GOD! Behold, I do not know how to speak, Because I am a youth." But the LORD said to me, "Do not say, 'I am a youth,' because everywhere I send you, you shall go, and all that I command you, you shall speak. Do not be afraid of them, for I am with you to deliver you," declares the LORD. Then the LORD stretched out His hand and touched my mouth, and the LORD said to me, "Behold, I have put My words in your mouth. See, I have appointed you this day over the nations and over the kingdoms, to pluck up and to break down, to destroy and to overthrow, to build and to plant." (Jer. 1:4–10)

The call and commissioning of Jeremiah is such an important passage of Scripture. Jeremiah was a priest, and now God was calling him to be a prophet to speak for Him.

In spite of great difficulty, much sorrow, and incredible opposition, Jeremiah faithfully stayed in that post as God's spokesman for the next forty years. It wasn't what you'd call a fun career. He had a harsh message of judgment and destruction that was coming from the hand of God to His people for all their disobedience, sin, idolatry, and spiritual adultery.

If Jeremiah had been on cable TV in those days, his ratings would have been almost zero. Nobody wanted to hear that message. It wasn't a popular theme, to say the least. You could say that his words were "politically incorrect" a couple thousand years before the term was ever invented. Nevertheless, God had told him, "This is what I want you to do," and Jeremiah did it. Difficult as his life and ministry may have been in those extraordinary days of national crisis and judgment, you and I can learn a great deal from Jeremiah about our own calling—and God's plan and purpose for our lives.

We'll talk more about Jeremiah momentarily, but first let's look at three certainties found in this passage of Scripture. I believe these certainties will help you deal with frustration and encourage you to find your purpose in life.

Certainty #1: God Knows All About You

"Before I formed you in the womb, I knew you."

Jeremiah 1:5

Hundreds of years earlier, King David had written, "O Lord, you have examined my heart and know everything about me" (Ps. 139:1 nlt).

In both passages, the Bible uses the same word for "know." It's a Hebrew term, *yada*, which means "to know in an intimate, personal way." The King James uses that same word, *know* or *knew*, to refer to a sexual relationship between a man and a woman. In Genesis 4:1, we read: "And Adam knew Eve his wife; and she conceived, and bare Cain."

God says to us, "I know you. I know you in an intimate, personal way." And David, by inspiration of the Spirit, echoed that truth by saying, "Lord, you . . . know everything about me."

Does the Lord really know everything *about you?*

Yes, everything.

He Knows All Your Days

God knows all your "days." Before you were ever born, God knew how many days there would be for you. And at this very moment, He knows exactly how many days, hours, and seconds you have left in your life. David wrote: "You saw me before I was born. Every day of my life was recorded in your book. Every moment was laid out before a single day had passed" (Ps. 139:16 NLT).

Isn't that amazing? God knows everything! And when He was knitting you together, as the scripture says, in your mother's womb (v. 13), He already knew when you would step out of this life and into the next. Down to the millisecond.

Some years ago, I led a funeral for Debbie's great-aunt Pearl. She lived to be ninety-six years, ten months, and twenty-four days old. She lived a long, full life, and before she was ever born, God knew she would. He had ordained for Pearl to live exactly ninety-six years, ten months, and twenty-four days.

Our lives, after all, are comprised of only so much time, only so many days. That's why Moses said in Psalm 90:12, "So teach us to number our days, that we may present to You a heart of wisdom." In the book of Ephesians, the Bible tells us: "Therefore be careful how you walk, not as unwise men but as wise, making the most of your time, because the days are evil" (5:15–16).

Killing time is really committing suicide by degrees. We don't need to kill time; we need to redeem the time. We need to make the most of the time God has given us because life is made up of a limited number of days . . . and God knew how many you will have before you were even born.

He Knows All Your Ways

Not only does God know all your days; He also knows all your *ways*. David wrote: "You scrutinize my path and my lying down, and are intimately acquainted with all my ways" (Ps. 139:3).

Before you ever entered this world, before your own parents had ever made your acquaintance, God knew in detail what you would be like. He knew your physical characteristics, your personality traits, your strengths and weaknesses, your likes and dislikes—and how they would change through the years. He knew that I would like spinach and broccoli, but hate beets. He knew I would cheer for the burnt orange of the University of Texas while I was being formed in my mother's womb in West Covina, California.

How does He know all those things? Because He is your all-wise Creator. He knows what you're like, what you're passionate about, what makes you tick . . . and what ticks you off. He put all that in there. He knows all your ways. He knew when He made me that I would be all thumbs with tools and mechanical things. He knew that would be part of my wiring, as well as all the strengths and talents He would graciously place within me.

And you know what is really cool? The God who knows everything about you, all your days and all your ways, all the good *and* bad things about you . . . loves you still. He knows every fault and failure, yet He still thinks you are terrific—worth dying for, as a matter of fact. Wow! Thank You, Lord.

And that leads us to the next certainty.

CERTAINTY #2: GOD HAS A SPECIAL PLAN FOR YOU

In Jeremiah 29:11 we read: "'For I know the plans that I have for you,' declares the LORD; 'plans for welfare and not for calamity, to give you a future and a hope.'" From the beginning it was very obvious that God had a distinct and specific plan for young Jeremiah's life: "Before I formed you in the womb I knew you," God had told him. "And before you were born I consecrated you; I have appointed you a prophet to the nations" (v. 5). In other words, *"Jeremiah, I set you apart way before I ever made you. Yes, you're a priest, but I have now appointed you as a prophet to the nations."*

Isn't a priest and a prophet pretty much the same thing?

No, not at all. This was definitely a huge stretch for Jeremiah. Priests performed the service of the temple, offered sacrifices, and involved themselves in many of the externals of worship. The prophet, however, spoke for God. He spent time alone with God, received His very words, and declared them to the people. By calling him to be a prophet, God was saying to Jeremiah, *"I want you to speak to the hearts of My people."* Sixty-six times in the book of Jeremiah, the Bible talks about the heart, and that was Jeremiah's ministry: to speak to the hearts of a cynical, stiff-necked, and rebellious people.

Oh, but it wasn't going to be easy. As mentioned earlier, he wasn't given the privilege of speaking bright, happy, positive messages that would build up his listeners. He wasn't promising Israel "your best life now." In fact, he was commissioned to tell God's people that they had wandered far off the path of God's intentions and were heading straight into catastrophic judgment if they didn't turn their hearts back to Him.

That was God's special, specific plan for Jeremiah.

But He also has a special, specific plan for you.

God's Special Plan for You

"'For I know the plans I have for you,' declares the Lord." Are you living out your own special plan from God? You say, "Well, how would I know? I don't know what the plan *is*. God hasn't come to me and told me in so many words, like He did with Jeremiah. God told him, 'I'm going to make you a prophet to the nations.' That was

pretty clear. Jeremiah didn't have to scratch his head and wonder about what God had in mind for him."

Although it may seem like it at times, finding God's will for your life is not a shell game. Have you ever seen an illusionist play the shell game? He has three coconut shells, and he places a little ball underneath one of them. Next, he shifts those shells really fast, moving the shell with the ball first this way, then that. Finally, he says, "Okay, guess which shell the ball is under." And you might think you've tracked every movement of that little ball, but when he lifts up the shell, it isn't where you thought it would be.

Is that what God does with us? When you pray, "Lord, what do You want me to do?" does He purposely make His will difficult to find? Think about it for a moment: Could anyone ever know the will of God if He played the shell game? No. If a master illusionist can make it next to impossible to find the ball, how much more could the Master of the universe keep us in the dark regarding His will for our lives if He so chose.

Stop trying to cram your round peg into a square hole! That kind of living produces tons of frustration.

The truth of the matter is this: God does *not* play the shell game! He *wants* us to know His will . . . and do it! The God who knows everything there is to know about you wants to put you into just the right spot, where you will fit perfectly.

Have you ever used the heel of your shoe as a hammer? When I was a kid, my mom would do that all the time. She would say, "Take off your shoe, Jeff; I need to hang this picture." And then—*bang, bang, bang*—she'd drive that little nail into the wall. Why did she do it that way? Because she didn't want to bother with finding a hammer when I (and my shoe) happened to be near at hand.

That's all right, I suppose, but can you imagine carrying a shoe to a construction site? Guys all around you have their carpenter's belts with their big hammers and power hammers, and you've got your shoe.

"What are you doing?" someone asks. And you say, "I'm ready to go to work and pound some nails." "Well, where is your hammer?" your coworker asks incredulously. "Hammer? Why do I need a hammer when I've got a good, solid shoe?" How foolish.

If God made you to be a shoe as you go through life, then don't be hammering nails. Hit the dance floor! Or kick field goals. Do something that a shoe was intended to do. Stop trying to cram your round peg into a square hole! That kind of living produces tons of frustration.

You say, "Well, Jeff, how can I figure out what I was made to do? How can I know God's will for my life?" What a great question. Let me give you three answers to help you find the round hole for your round peg.

1. God's will is revealed when we diligently seek Him.

"You will seek Me and find Me when you search for Me with all your heart."

JEREMIAH 29:13

What a wonderful promise from God. If you will diligently seek after God, faithfully call on His name, and discipline yourself to spend time in His Word daily, God promises, *"You'll find Me."*

It's not a shell game. It's not tearing apart a haystack to find that proverbial little needle. But it *is* a matter of diligence, patience, faithfulness, and surrendering yourself to the Lord and His purposes day by day. This, by the way, is a process that will weed out those who aren't truly serious about knowing and following God's will. He reveals His heart and His ways to those who *diligently* seek Him.

If you seek and find God, you will also find what He wants you to do.

2. God's will is revealed when we humbly submit to Him.

> *The question is this: Do we really want what He wants for our lives, or do we want Him to simply rubber-stamp our plans and desires?*

Jesus said, "If any man is willing to do His will, he shall know of the teaching, whether it is of God" (John 7:17). That's a great principle. Are you ready and willing to do what God wants you to do? If so, then He promises to tell you.

The question is this: Do we really want what He wants for our lives, or do we want Him to simply rubber-stamp *our* plans and desires? Do we come to Him with our minds already made up, merely asking for His blessing? Do we say, "Lord, I will do this, but I *won't* do that, and I *won't* go there."

If that's the way we approach God, wanting Him to rubber-stamp our plans, we really can't expect to receive His will for our lives. God says, *"I don't own a rubber stamp, so I'm not going to rubber-stamp your will. But if you're willing to do My will, then I will reveal it to you."*

Bill Bright is a household name in Christian circles. Dr. Bright came to Christ when he was in his twenties, and God led him to found Campus Crusade on the campus of UCLA in the 1950s.

During that time, he wrote a little booklet called, *Have You Heard of the Four Spiritual Laws?* This little tract, featuring the plan of salvation, has been given out to more than 2.5 billion people. When Dr. Bright died in 2003, Campus Crusade had twenty-six thousand paid staff, plus tens of thousands of volunteers. It is said that he was involved in the salvation of more than 100 million people.

When Pastor Rick Warren interviewed Dr. Bright, he asked him, "Why did God use and bless your life so much?"

He said, 'When I was a young man I made a contract with God. I literally wrote it out and signed my name at the bottom. It read, 'From this day forward, I am a slave of Jesus Christ.'" Bill surrendered to God and he agreed to it in writing.

Dr. Bright went on to say, "We've [he and his wife, Vonette] been slaves now for fifty some years, and I must tell you it's the most liberating thing that's ever happened to me." And why was it so liberating? Because as a slave, Bill Bright understood that his only job was to obey the Master. All the worries and cares of his life were God's concern, not Bill's.

Amen! Without question, God will reveal His will to those who fully submit to Him and say, "Lord, I am willing to be Your servant, to be Your slave, to go wherever You want me to go and do whatever You want me to do." God will answer that kind of prayer by revealing His will. And you can take that to the bank!

3. GOD'S WILL IS REVEALED WHEN WE SIMPLY DELIGHT IN HIM.

Psalm 34:8 says, "O taste and see that the LORD is good." Psalm 37:4 adds, "Delight yourself in the LORD; and He will give you the desires of your heart."

Our God is a good God, and He wants you to delight in Him.

A relationship with God isn't like getting a vaccination in your shoulder or swallowing bad-tasting medicine in order to get well. In fact, it's the most wonderful experience in all of life. I *enjoy* my relationship with God. I *delight* in knowing Him and talking to Him and being with Him.

Is your heart like soft clay or hard clay? Do you listen carefully for the voice of the Holy Spirit and quickly yield to His touch on your life?

It is important to note that the Hebrew word for "delight" in Psalm 37:4 literally means "to be soft, to be pliable." God is saying, *"Make yourself soft and pliable in My hands. Don't allow yourself to become hard or unyielding or inflexible"*. In Jeremiah 18, the Lord led Jeremiah to the potter's house as he was working on the wheel. God's purpose in that field trip was to teach an important object lesson: God is the Potter, and we are the clay. If we will delight in Him, making ourselves soft and pliable in the Potter's hands, then He will give us the desires of our hearts.

I know from personal experience that when a potter is working on the wheel, soft clay is a must. If the clay is soft, the potter barely has to nudge it to get it to move in the desired direction. Hard clay, on the other hand, becomes virtually impossible to shape because it refuses to yield to the potter's wishes.

Is your heart like soft clay or hard clay? Do you listen carefully for the voice of the Holy Spirit and quickly yield to His touch on your life? Or does the Lord have to exert tons of pressure on you (and possibly break you in the process) just to get your attention? Ask God to make you soft in His hands. When you're soft, you get to experience the desires of your heart.

What are those desires? What are the dreams in your heart? So often when we talk about finding God's will, we immediately think of something negative. We imagine that if we signed a contract with the Lord, as Bill Bright did, God would immediately ship us off to the middle of some jungle, where we would live in a mud hut, drink water out of a dirty puddle, be plagued with constant diarrhea, and end up marrying some native girl who has a bone through her nose and earlobes down to her shoulders.

We laugh at that sentiment, but the truth of the matter is, we so often think negatively when we think of the will of God. Listen, God's will is *not* something terrible for you. It is something wonderful.

Years ago, I went to Kenya on a mission trip. The missionary we worked with in Kenya was from the United States. He was a delightful man named Clay. Contrary to our oftentimes warped beliefs, Clay did not live in a mud hut; neither was his wife sporting a bone in her nose. (I did not ask him about his digestive tract.)

Clay had a calling on his life to work with the people of Kenya. He successfully served in Kenya for thirty years, planting hundreds of churches and leading untold thousands to faith in Christ. Did he do this work reluctantly? Was he constantly wishing he could be somewhere else? No! He loved being in Kenya. His heart was knit to that place and those people. He wanted to serve in Kenya more than any place in the world. It was God's special plan for his life, and Clay loved it!

God calls people to do all sorts of different things. If your heart is caught up with God and His will, you will be overjoyed living where God wants you to live, doing what He has called you to do. Living with a sense of purpose, calling, and direction fills your heart to overflowing and causes frustration to melt away like a snow cone in Phoenix.

If you delight yourself in the Lord, He *will* give you the desires of your heart. In other words, He will plant His dreams and desires deep within you, so that you want them more than anything else.

But don't imagine being a missionary in Africa (or a preacher in Texas) is somehow better or more sacred than some calling in the secular world. The key is to be content where He has placed you. Martin Luther once said, "A dairymaid can milk cows to the glory of God."

Life is too short and too precious to just work and work and work and work at a job you don't like, simply because it pays well.

Years ago I had a urologist named Dr. E. C. Winkel. His office maxim read, "If you can't tinkle, come see Winkel." (And I am not kidding. It was printed on his business card.) Well, God had just called me into the ministry at that time, and I was talking to Dr. Chip Winkel—E. C.'s son and partner in the practice—about God's will and purpose for our lives. He said to me, "Jeff, you might think I'm crazy, but I believe God has called me to be a urologist."

"I don't think that's crazy at all," I said. "I think God calls people to be bankers and accountants and sales reps and homemakers and teachers and coaches. I think He has different plans for everybody." He knows the plans He has for us, and they are good plans.

What has God called you to do? What dream is in your heart? If every job paid the same, what would you be doing? Would you still do what you're doing now?

Life is too short and too precious to just work and work and work and work at a job you don't like, simply because it pays well.

What does God have for you to do? Ask Him! Begin to delight yourself in Him, and then watch for His leading. God wants you to be fulfilled. He knows all about you, and He has a special plan for you.

CERTAINTY #3: GOD WILL EQUIP
YOU TO ACCOMPLISH HIS PLAN

When the Lord first called Jeremiah to be a prophet to the nations, the lad probably groaned out loud. In Jeremiah 1:6, he said to the Lord, "Alas, Lord GOD! Behold, I do not know how to speak, because I am a youth." In other words, "God, I don't know how this happened, but I think You've got the wrong guy. You dialed the wrong number. I'm not able to do this. I'm inexperienced. I don't know how to speak. I haven't taken any oratory classes. I'm not a prophet; I'm a priest. There's no way, God, that I can do what you are asking me to do."

That's when God assured this young man that He would equip him with everything he needed to accomplish His purpose and plan. Look how the Lord answered Jeremiah:

> The LORD replied, "Don't say, 'I'm too young,' for you must go wherever I send you and say whatever I tell you. And don't be afraid of the people, for I will be with you and will protect you. I, the LORD, have spoken!" (Jer. 1:7–8 NLT)

How does God equip? First of all, He equips with His presence. *"I will be with you and will protect you."*

Second, God equips with His protection. He was going to take care of Jeremiah and deliver him. God told Jeremiah, *"You're going to preach a message, and it's not going to be an easy message, but I will be right there at your side to protect you."* In verse 10, the Lord said that Jeremiah's message would have this effect: "to pluck up and to break down, to destroy and to overthrow." He would be preaching judgment, and believe me, people did *not* want to hear that. In fact, they would eventually try to silence the young prophet—beating him, jailing him, even trying to kill him.

At one point in his ministry, Jeremiah told the Lord, "I've become a laughingstock. Everywhere I go, people make fun of me. But what can I do? Every time I open my mouth, all I can share is Your message of destruction and judgment. That's what comes out! I wish I had a different sermon, but You have put Your message deep down in my heart, and it's like a fire burning within me. If I try to stay quiet and keep my mouth shut, then Your word just burns in my bones and I have to let it out, even though everyone hates it and hates me" (Jer. 20:7–9, paraphrased).

The fact is, God didn't put us here to please one another. We're here to please Him. He's the One who matters. And He wasn't going to let anyone hurt His prophet until he had said everything God had given him to say.

Finally, God will equip you with His provision. In Jeremiah 1:9, we read: "Then the LORD stretched out His hand and touched my mouth, and the LORD said to me, 'Behold, I have put My words in your mouth.'" That's what every prophet—and preacher—needs. He needs God's words in his mouth, so he's not just speaking on his own, but he's saying what God has told him to say.

Have you ever been to a church service and found yourself thinking thoughts like these: *I wonder if that speaker has spent time with God. I really don't know if he's speaking the words of God. I think he might just be saying stuff that comes from his own mind.* That can make for a pretty long sermon, can't it? It seems as if it will never end as the speaker rambles on and on, sharing his own thoughts and opinions.

It's different when the speaker or pastor has spent time with the Lord. He may not be the best orator in the world, but there's something about the words that touches your soul. And when he says, "Thus says the Lord," you really believe him.

That's what God did for Jeremiah. The Lord put force and power behind the prophet's words, and here we are, thousands of years later, still reading them, still being moved by them. Jeremiah could never have done that on his own. He needed the Lord's provision.

What does God have for you to do? What calling does He have on your life? What are the desires He has placed deep down in your soul? Maybe the idea of "stepping out of the boat" frightens you a little . . . or a lot! Maybe you find yourself thinking, *I feel in my heart that God wants me to do so-and-so, but that would mean moving to a new city, or leaving my job, or a big change in direction. What about my finances? How would I manage it? Maybe I'm too old [or too young] to be thinking of these things. It just doesn't seem like I can do it.*

The Lord says, "Quit saying you can't. I never said you could. I said that I would. So start trusting Me."

The Lord says, "*Quit saying you can't. I never said* you *could. I said that* I *would. So start trusting Me.*" In Philippians 4:19 the apostle Paul wrote: "And my God will supply all your needs according to His riches in glory in Christ Jesus." You may have heard this before, but it's just as true as it ever was: *Where God guides, God supplies.* He will meet your needs, just as He did for Jeremiah.

My Call

In the life-changing Bible study *Experiencing God*, Dr. Henry Blackaby speaks of "a holy restlessness"[3] that the Lord uses in the lives of people to move them to a new direction and a new calling. No doubt, the "holy restlessness" is coupled with frustration as

God begins to change the course of a life. I know about this "holy restlessness" and frustration all too well, as God used both in my life when I was in my early thirties.

I had graduated from college with a business degree, was married with three girls, and had a job selling water treatment chemicals for Nalco Chemical Company in Houston, Texas. The job was roughly divided between sales and technical work. Most of the guys I worked with were chemical or mechanical engineers.

As I've already confessed, "technical" isn't really my cup of tea. I can still remember working with one of my customers as he told me of problems he was having with his water treatment controller. "This controller is on the fritz," he said. "There seems to be an electrical power issue. Can you fix it?"

As I stood in front of that malfunctioning controller, my first thought was, *Man, if I had this situation at my house, I'd call a service guy.* And then it struck me. *Wait . . . I am the service guy!*

I knew I was in trouble. I just kept praying, "Dear God, don't let me electrocute myself."

My job at Nalco paid well and had great benefits. I worked hard and was successful, but I really didn't like it all that much. In truth, I was a round peg working overtime trying to fit into a square hole.

While I was working at Nalco, I began teaching a Sunday school class at our church. And as much as I hated technical work, I *loved* teaching the Bible. It was all I could think about. As I drove around to different locations in my company car, I kept teaching and reteaching my Sunday school lesson for the week in my mind, getting more and more excited the closer it got to Sunday. My heart was just brimming over with God's Word and the desire to share it.

After about five years of this, I heard a message about the apostle Peter walking on water, and how he had to come to the place where he was willing "to step out of the boat." And the preacher, my friend

Dr. Rich Halcombe, kept saying, "What is God calling you to do? What is the dream He has placed in your heart? What does God want for your future? What have you been so afraid to say yes to?"

My desire was ministry; with everything in me, that's what I longed to do. And that night, at that Wednesday evening service, I got down on my knees at the invitation time and said, "Lord, I believe You're calling me to preach. And God, I commit my life to doing just that."

When I said those words to God, it was as if He pulled me close to His heart and said these unforgettable words: *"Jeff, I've been waiting for you to make that decision. Now we've got a deal."*

I remember going home and telling Debbie about it. I can't say that she was on board right away with the idea of a radical change in direction, but as time went by, the Lord spoke to her heart too. About a year later, I resigned from my high-paying job with great benefits and a company car, and we moved to North Carolina where I would go to seminary. I had eight thousand dollars in the bank, no job, and a wife and three kids to support. I remember thinking, *God, this would have been a whole lot easier if You had called me straight out of college. Then I was free as a bird and didn't have all these responsibilities.* And the Lord seemed to reply, *"Be quiet, boy. Just obey Me. I know exactly what I'm doing."*

I'd been in seminary for approximately one year when my former pastor, Dr. Damon Shook, called me. At that time, he was senior pastor of my home church, Champion Forest Baptist Church in Houston. He said, "Jeff, I'd like to talk to you about coming on staff at Champion Forest. You can be my assistant, and I will teach you how to be a pastor. You can go to seminary here; I'll give you opportunities to preach and provide you with training."

Talk about God giving you the desires of your heart! I couldn't have asked for a better situation than that. Within two years of saying yes to the Lord, I was preaching before a large congregation at my home church, and loving every minute of it.

To be honest with you, I don't have the "nowhere man" syndrome anymore. I know that I'm a puzzle piece God has placed into the right slot, and that gives me great fulfillment and satisfaction. Yes, I still get frustrated when I try to repair things around the house. And I get frustrated watching the Texas Longhorns blow opportunities and lose games they should have won. I still have *that* sort of frustration from time to time, but I don't have the frustration that says, "I'm going nowhere and making zero difference in my life."

When you're where God wants you to be, your life is fulfilling and you *know* you're making a difference—whether that's being a stay-at-home mom or a real estate agent or a chef or an accountant or a missionary. If that's what God wants you to do and where God wants you to be, there's no better place for you in the whole world.

Let me encourage you to take some time right now to soberly evaluate your life. How is your frustration level? Are you feeling the deadly combination of anger and discouragement? Be honest: Are you doing what God wants you and created you to do?

I know the thought of a move or a career change is frightening, but if God is truly leading you to step out of the boat and make a change, you won't be sorry. People with regrets are not those who stepped out in faith; they are the ones who didn't.

You can silence the blaring smoke alarm of frustration as you get in on the plan God has for you. As a wise man once said, "Life's greatest discovery is finding the will of God, and life's greatest satisfaction is doing the will of God." So, start today.

FOUR

WORRY

When Anxiety Attacks

Don't worry about anything. . . .

PHILIPPIANS 4:6 NLT

R ecently I heard about a company enduring a very bumpy road financially. Everyone knew that layoffs were coming. As a result, the employees were very worried about their jobs.

Because the staff had become so afraid and preoccupied, morale had slipped in this company . . . and so had productivity. "What's going to happen? Will we shut down? Will I be one of those who gets the ax?"

When the big boss came into town, he could tell the mood had become very negative. On his arrival, he quickly called a meeting with all his department heads. "The morale around here is terrible. We can't go on like this, with everyone so anxious and fearful," he said. "We need to lighten up the mood. We need a little humor around here. Humor is the ticket to lift the morale."

Then the boss looked over at the sales manager. "Operation Humor; let's start with you," he said.

"Okay," the manager replied.

The boss said, "Knock, knock."

The manager countered, "Who's there?"

"Not *you* anymore!"

As you can imagine, Operation Humor didn't produce the desired results for that company.

Maybe in these current economic times, that story hits a little too close to home. But the truth of the matter is this: worry is something all of us have to deal with, probably every day.

WORRY DEFINED

The word *worry* comes from the old Anglo-Saxon word *wyrgan*, which means "to strangle." *Wyrgan* is what happens when a dog gets hold of a shoe. Have you ever watched a dog with an old shoe? He gets that piece of footwear in his teeth and violently shakes it from side to side. If you try to extract it from his mouth, he will pull all the harder, growling and jerking his head back and forth, trying to keep his hold. And that is a vivid picture of worry . . . and what it does to your soul. It's like a dog that has his teeth embedded in your thoughts and emotions, and he's just pulling at you, chewing on you, and trying to tear you apart. That's what it's like to live with anxiety and worry.

In seminary class, Dr. McDill taught this insightful definition of worry: "the tension and distress experienced over the anticipated loss, whether real or imagined, of some valued possession." We've all felt that, haven't we? It's when you find yourself obsessing over the possible loss of some possession of yours that you truly treasure, whether it's your child, your job, your marriage, your future, your finances, or your health.

> Worry: *the tension and distress experienced over the anticipated loss, whether real or imagined, of some valued possession.*

Are you worried today as you read these words? Does it feel as though something has its teeth in your soul, pulling you back and forth? Maybe you're worried about a medical test. You went to the doctor last week, and now you're waiting for the lab reports. You think to yourself, *Oh no. What if I have some serious disease?* Perhaps you're worried because your job is in jeopardy, or because your finances seem to be evaporating before your eyes. Or maybe you're worried over a child who is making terrible life choices. We have all sorts of possible worries, don't we?

If you let it, worry will steal your sleep, tie your stomach in knots, dominate your thinking, and cast a cloud of fear over everything in your life. Dr. Charles Mayo of the Mayo Clinic said, "Worry affects the circulation, the heart, the glands, and the entire nervous system."[1] Put another way, worry will do to your physical body and your emotional makeup what sand will do to your car's gas tank. It will gum up the works and choke out the operation.

THE REAL PROBLEM

What is the real issue with worry? What is the smoke-alarm message in that miserable emotion? The message is this: Your God-given sense of security is on fire. You anticipate the loss of something you value, and worry has you tied up like a mass of gnarled fishing line.

EMOTION: Worry
WARNING: Your God-given sense of security is on fire.

So how can you silence the blaring smoke alarm of worry? Is it possible for you to complete this chapter and close this book with peace, not worried and anxious about a thing?

Believe it or not, it is.

And the Lord has some strong answers for your worries and anxieties in His famous Sermon on the Mount:

No one can serve two masters; for either he will hate the one and love the other, or he will be devoted to one and despise the other. You cannot serve God and wealth.

For this reason I say to you, do not be worried about your life, *as to* what you will eat or what you will drink; nor for your body, *as to* what you will put on. Is not life more than food, and the body more than clothing? Look at the birds of the air, that they do not sow, nor reap nor gather into barns, and *yet* your heavenly Father feeds them. Are you not worth much more than they? And who of you by being worried can add a *single* hour to his life? And why are you worried about clothing? Observe how the lilies of the field grow; they do not toil nor do they spin, yet I say to you that not even Solomon in all his glory clothed himself like one of these. But if God so clothes the grass of the field, which is *alive* today and tomorrow is thrown into the furnace, *will He* not much more *clothe* you? You of little faith! Do not worry then, saying, "What will we eat?" or "What will we drink?" or "What will we wear for clothing?" For the Gentiles eagerly seek all these things; for your heavenly Father knows that you need all these things. But seek first His kingdom and His righteousness, and all these things will be added to you.

So do not worry about tomorrow; for tomorrow will care for itself. Each day has enough trouble of its own. (Matt. 6:24–34)

> *Three times in ten verses Jesus emphatically says, "Do not be worried . . . do not be worried . . . do not worry."*

Three times in ten verses Jesus emphatically says, "*Do not be worried . . . do not be worried . . . do not worry.*" Don't be worried about your life. Don't be worried about your provisions. Don't be worried about tomorrow. In fact, the Lord has a three-part action plan for you that will enable you to silence that *worry* alarm in your soul and reclaim the peace and tranquility He intends for His sons and daughters.

PART ONE: TRUST GOD TO TAKE CARE OF YOU

Part one of the three-part action plan is to put your trust into action. Just trust God to take care of you. How simple is that?

When Jesus originally preached this sermon, His audience was made up of common, everyday folks. They weren't wealthy aristocrats, living in palatial mansions. They were mostly farmers who were concerned with the weather, their crops, and an oppressive government that taxed what little profit they might eke from the soil or vineyards. As a result, they would worry about things like, "What shall we eat, and what shall we drink, and with what shall we clothe ourselves?" In other words, they worried about the basic necessities of life. Most of us probably haven't worried too much today about food, water, clothing, and shelter. But even though we're not necessarily worried about our next meal, we may truly be anxious about our next car payment or our next mortgage payment.

Regardless of what specific thing you're worried about, worry is still worry—a corrosive force in our lives that eats away at our sense of security. And God says, "What you need to do is trust Me to take care of you."

Learn from the Birds

Regardless of what specific thing you're worried about, worry is still worry—a corrosive force in our lives that eats away at our sense of security. And God says, *"What you need to do is trust Me to take care of you."*

Jesus said, "Look at the birds." Birds don't concern themselves with planting, weeding, and reaping. They're not farmers. They're not thinking, *Oh my, oh my, I have to get my ground plowed, and then make sure I plant my seed, and be ready to harvest at the right time.* Birds don't do any of that stuff. They don't have a pantry in the nest or a freezer in the garage. They don't have a six-month emergency food supply in the basement. They don't have grain silos or barns or even Tupperware containers. And they don't worry about it, either. They just go out every day to gather what God provides.

Arguing from the lesser to the greater, the Lord concluded, *"Listen. If I feed the birds, how much more am I going to feed you? If I clothe the lilies of the field in tremendous splendor—more so than Solomon ever clothed himself—and those little flowers are alive today and thrown into the furnace tomorrow, how much more will I do for you?"*

In verse 30, He summed it up with these convicting words, "You of little faith."

Maybe we don't like to think of it this way, but worry is really nothing more than practical atheism.

At its core, worry is a faith issue, because when you boil it down, worry is the opposite of faith.

George Mueller once observed, "The beginning of anxiety is the *end* of *faith*, and the beginning of true *faith* is the *end* of anxiety."[2] When you stop trusting God, you begin to worry, because worry and faith are polar opposites.

Maybe we don't like to think of it this way, but worry is really nothing more than practical atheism. Atheism says, "I don't believe there is a God." No Christian would be guilty of atheism, foolishly *believing* there is no God. But many Christians are guilty of practical atheism, foolishly *living* as if there is no God to care for His children. How tragic, yet how commonplace.

Worry isn't just an annoyance or a weakness or a "little failing"—it is *sin*. In Romans 14:23, Paul declared that "whatever is not from faith is sin." And if you're not trusting God, then you're not walking and living by faith.

I heard a story about a little boy who went with his granddad to see a farm, and that day the farmer was killing chickens. He would take a chicken, put its head on a chopping block, and—whack!—cut off its head with a hatchet. The little boy had never seen anything like this in his life. He had only seen chicken in a plastic wrapper from the store, or maybe in a Colonel Sanders bucket. He was thoroughly amazed to see a chicken get its head cut off, then begin to flail about and run around for a while before it dropped over to lie still.

After observing this strange phenomenon for about ten minutes, the little boy said triumphantly to his grandfather, "Hey, Granddad, I think I've got this figured out. The chickens don't mind it so much once they get used to it."

That's the way we are with our worries. We've gotten used to them. We live with worry like living with a pebble in our shoe. Yes, it's uncomfortable, and yes, it gives me blisters and makes me limp sometimes. But it's only a little pebble. "It's no big deal. I can live with it," you say. Don't kid yourself. Practical atheism is a big deal.

So many people would never think of worry as a sin. After all, it's not murder or adultery or stealing or taking God's name in vain. It didn't make the Big 10 that God gave to Moses on Mount Sinai. But it is still sin, and a sin for which Jesus had to suffer and die. And it still causes a break in our fellowship with the Lord.

Did it ever occur to you what our persistent worry says to God? Actually, it tells Him three heartbreaking things.

1. WORRY SAYS TO GOD, "YOU MUST NOT BE AWARE OF MY SITUATION."

"Lord, You must have misplaced my file, or You're busy with someone else. Or maybe You went on vacation. Or maybe Your GPS is on the fritz, because You don't seem to know where I am or what I'm going through. You're not aware of the situation in my office. You're not up to speed on my troubles at home. You're not up-to-date on my latest health report. God, where are You?"

In Psalm 139, however, David wrote:

> *You know when I sit down and when I rise up;*
> *You understand my thought from afar.*
> *You scrutinize my path and my lying down,*
> *And are intimately acquainted with all my ways.*
> *Even before there is a word on my tongue,*
> *Behold, O LORD, You know it all. (vv. 2–4)*

In reference to our frequent worries over physical needs, Jesus said in Matthew 6:32, "Your heavenly Father knows that you need all these things." Listen, my friend, God knows what's going on. He's not oblivious. He's not distracted. He's not losing you on His radar screen. If a little sparrow doesn't even fall to the ground apart from God's knowledge and permission, then He certainly knows every particular of your life.

As a matter of fact, Jesus said that the very hairs of your head are numbered. Did you catch that? God doesn't just *know* the number of hairs on your head; He actually numbers each one. Pull a hair out and look at it. Go ahead—do it. As

The point is, God is aware of everything going on in your life. From the mammoth to the minute, He knows it all.

you look at that individual hair, know this: God knows the number of that hair. Perhaps you pulled out number 806 of 7,540 hairs. (The other day, I pulled out number 6 of 10.) The point is, God is aware of *everything* going on in your life. From the mammoth to the minute, He knows it all.

2. WORRY SAYS TO GOD, "YOU MUST NOT CARE ABOUT MY SITUATION."

"All right, Lord, I agree that You must know everything. You even know all there is to know about my situation. But since You're not helping me, I have to conclude that while You know, You must not really care because You're not willing to assist me."

Have you ever looked at God's perceived lack of action on your behalf and silently surmised that God must not care about you? I have . . . and that thought is a complete lie. All of Scripture proves and declares that God not only knows the circumstances of our lives in great detail, but in His love, He deeply cares. Peter said it most clearly: "Cast all your anxiety on him *because he cares for you*" (1 Peter 5:7 NIV; emphasis added).

The gospel of Matthew gives us this tender account: "A leper came to [Jesus] and bowed down before Him, and said, 'Lord, if You are willing, You can make me clean.' Jesus stretched out His hand and touched him, saying, 'I am willing. Be cleansed.' And immediately his leprosy was cleansed" (8:2–3).

God is willing to help us. He is aware. And He does care. The nail scars in His hands and feet prove it.

3. WORRY SAYS TO GOD, "YOU MUST NOT BE ABLE IN THIS SITUATION."

This may be the most preposterous notion of all. Yet that's exactly what our constant worry/anxiety says to God. We're saying, "All right, Lord, I do think You are aware of what I'm going through, and my heart tells me You must care for me (at least a little). But I'm beginning to think You don't have the power to make a difference. This situation has gone on so long and become such a tangled mess that I don't think even You can turn it around."

What a terrible thought! It borders on blasphemy, as it subconsciously tells the God who spoke the worlds into existence that we think He is too puny and too powerless to meet our pressing financial, physical, or relational needs.

A story is told of two birds on a tree branch in the park, listening in on a conversation between a husband and wife. This couple was in obvious distress, wringing their hands as they talked about a coming layoff at work. They groaned over the fact that they weren't going to have the finances to make it. And then they went on and on about the problems with their kids and their worries about the future.

One of the birds just shook his little head. "Isn't it sad," he said to the other bird, "that they don't have a heavenly Father to take care of them like we do?"

GOD IS ABLE

In the book of Isaiah, the Lord used an interesting expression. He said to Israel, "Was my arm too short to ransom you? Do I lack the strength to rescue you? . . . Surely the arm of the LORD is not too short to save" (50:2; 59:1 NIV).

In other words, God's arms are plenty long enough to reach you, touch you, and help you in your need. You will never find God short-armed or short-handed.

Is God able to take care of you and me? *Are you kidding?* This is the God of whom it is said: "Now to Him who is able to do far more abundantly beyond all that we ask or think, according to the power that works within us, to Him be the glory" (Eph. 3:20–21).

God is able. He is more than able. In any situation you're in, He says, *"I'm able. I can handle this. Look to Me, and put your trust in Me. I will take care of you."* What's more, God loves it when we do that. He loves it when we bring all the broken pieces and splintered shards of our life situations and pour them onto His lap.

GOD CAN PART THE SEA

I recall writing a devotional one day and titling it "When You Get Between a Rock and a Hard Place." Remember when the children of Israel found themselves in that position? They were camped at the edge of the Red Sea, with Pharaoh and his troops closing in on them from behind with fiery retribution in their eyes.

So you've got the sea on one side, and your deadly enemy on the other. That's being between a rock and a hard place. Seeing their plight, the Israelites cried aloud in their fear and despair. I love the line in the old movie *The Ten Commandments*, when Pharaoh (portrayed by Yul Brynner) surveys the Israelites' helpless, hopeless situation and says in disdain, "Moses' God isn't much of a general."[3] Pharaoh

> *"Behold, I am the LORD, the God of all flesh; is anything too difficult for Me?" (Jer. 32:27)*

could easily see that God had led them to a dead end. There was no way out.

But there was a way out, wasn't there? A way no one expected. A way no one had foreseen or imagined. God opened the sea and led the Israelites through the divided waters to safety. That is God's specialty. He loves to make a way where there seems to be no way. He loves to use our dead-end, "rock and a hard place" situation to demonstrate His wisdom, power, and love. God had purposely led the Israelites to that impossible place in order to show them His might and His ability to care for them—no matter what.

In that moment, He was saying to them what He would say to the prophet Jeremiah centuries later: "Behold, I am the LORD, the God of all flesh; is anything too difficult for Me?" (Jer. 32:27).

TOO DIFFICULT FOR GOD?

Is your situation too difficult for God? Too complicated? Too tangled? Too messed up? Is anything—*anything*—in all the world too difficult for Him?

Earlier in the book, I wrote about God calling me into the ministry. And what I struggled with more than anything at that time was, How am I going to make it financially? I had just resigned from my job, and I had a family to support. How would I keep food on the table? How would I pay the mortgage? I was struggling big-time with worry.

"All worry is caused by calculating without God."
—Oswald Chambers

But guess what? It *wasn't* too difficult for God. He found a way to take care of me. Somehow, some way, He enabled me to study, work, and pay all the bills. Frankly, I will *never* forget those days. That was something of a Red Sea experience for me. I didn't see how He would do it, but I stepped out in obedience anyway, and He came through! I've reminded myself of that provision time and again in the months and years since. God is able to take care of anything that touches my life, or the life of my family.

Oswald Chambers said this: "All worry is caused by calculating without God."[4] In other words, before you begin to be anxious over something, you'd better make sure you've included the almighty God in your calculations.

When my kids were little, we taught them this song: "My God is so big, so strong, and so mighty. There's nothing my God cannot do."[5] It's a simple little song that is profoundly true! No matter what you're facing in life, remember that He can see you through it.

PART TWO: GIVE GOD OWNERSHIP OF ALL YOU POSSESS

Worry is very closely tied to what you possess, what belongs to you. As we've already noted, worry is the tension and distress experienced over the anticipated loss of some valued possession.

God's action plan for eliminating worry gives us a very simple solution for that problem: give all that you possess to Him.

When you think about it, God owns everything anyway. Psalm 24:1 says, "The earth is the LORD's and all it contains." So what part of "all" don't we understand? Our possessions are His. *We* are His.

When you leave this earth, how much of this world's goods do you get to take with you? Maybe you've heard the old expression, "I've never seen a hearse pulling a U-Haul." It's a ridiculous image, isn't it? There are no moving vans or Help-U-Move trucks rolling up in front of the funeral home or cemetery. When you leave this life, you leave *everything.* You leave behind all that you have . . . and take with you all that you are.

So why do we waste so much emotional energy worrying about possessions?

Philippians 4:6 says, "Be anxious for nothing." And what is nothing? It's actually two words: *no thing.* God is telling us here, *"Don't worry about 'things' at all. Don't worry about your possessions. Give those over to Me, because they really don't belong to you anyway."*

Let's imagine that some good friends of yours have left on a long vacation. Now honestly, do you find yourself worrying about someone breaking into their house? Do you lose sleep at night feeling anxious that their water heater might burst a pipe or that wood rats might sneak into their attic? Of course you don't! You may have prayed protection over their home as they departed, but then you put it out of your mind, and it doesn't concern you much at all. Why? Because it's *their* house and *their* stuff. Yes, they're your friends, but you trust them to take all the necessary precautions and make all the crucial provisions to protect their own home in their absence.

THE COMPANY CAR

When I worked in the business world, I had a company car, and I loved it. One of the greatest perks you can ever give somebody is a company car. It's great because you get to drive it, but it's not yours. It belongs to the company. And when that car needs maintenance, you take it into the shop, hand them the company credit card, and say, "Take care of it. Change the tires. Change the oil. Change the transmission fluid. Give it the works. Whatever is needed, do it."

If it had been my car, I may have driven a little farther on those tires with thin tread. If it had been mine, I may not have let them change the air filter because it had some dust in it. (I'm a penny pincher at heart.) But since it was the company's car, my attitude was a lot like Nike's—Just Do It. The company wanted their car in tip-top condition. You see, I did not fret over the company car . . . because it wasn't mine.

Everything in your life is like a company car. You don't own it, God does.

As a Christian, as someone who's been purchased with the precious blood of Jesus, and as someone who wants to experience God's peace, *everything in your life is a company car.* You don't own it, and it isn't your name that's on the title. God's name is on the title. He bought and paid for you. You get to use the car, enjoy the car, service the car, appreciate the car, and put all kinds of miles on the car, but it isn't your car. God owns it, and He is responsible to take care of what He owns . . . so you don't have to stress about it one little bit. God lets you manage some of His things, but they are always *His* things, not yours.

That is such a freeing concept! Let that sink into your heart, and it will change the way you think about life on this earth. Everything in my life is a company car. My wife is a company car. My kids are a company car. So are my house, my position at my church, my bank account, and my health. I get to care for and manage these things to a degree, but I don't own *any* of them. They belong to God, and He lets me use them.

Scripture brings this to the forefront in Matthew 25:14 when it says, "It is just like a man about to go on a journey, who called his own slaves and entrusted his possessions to them." That's what God has done with you and me. He's entrusted His possessions to us . . . for now. We don't own them. They're His. We just manage them.

THE WORRY SECRET

How, then, does worry come into our lives? Why do we hear that loud smoke alarm of over-the-top anxiety? It's simply because we have taken ownership of things that don't belong to us! We've somehow forgotten that the company car belongs to the company . . . and we are treating it as if it belongs to us. It doesn't. It never did. We own nothing. God owns everything.

So, what is the answer to worry? As best you can, give everything you have back to God. Put everything back in His hands. Step into the role of "manager" and remind yourself (again and again if you have to) that He is the owner. Everything we touch in this life, everything that we are, is on loan from Him.

WILL THAT EVER HAPPEN?

Besides that huge reality, much of what we worry about will never happen anyway. Somebody actually did a study of this once and concluded that 40 percent of the things we worry about will never happen.[6]

When I was in my early thirties, I began to notice a small lump on my forearm, about the size of a pea. When I would lift weights, doing curls and other exercises, it would poke out. *That's weird*, I thought. *What in the world is that?*

I told Debbie about it, and, good wife that she is, she said, "Jeff, you need to get that checked out." She's always been big on going to the doctor, and I've always looked for reasons *not* to. Nevertheless, she wanted me to go . . . for her peace of mind. So I called the doctor's office and set up an appointment.

The next day, as I was driving down the road in my company car (I just had to throw that in), I began to have these fearful thoughts: *What if that little lump is really something? What if it's cancer? Oh, my soul, maybe I do have cancer. I may have to have surgery. I may have to go through chemo. I might lose my hair.* (Okay, that wasn't really a concern.) *How will Debbie get along without me? Will she remarry? How will I tell the kids about this? Will they grow up without a daddy?*

So there I was, driving down the highway in Houston, feeling as if my life were already over. I almost choked up visualizing my own funeral. The little lump that was probably nothing had caused me to project the worst and start planning my memorial service.

As it turned out, that little lump was nothing but some fatty tissue. They cut it out right there in the office, and that was that. But who knows how long I allowed my stomach to be tied up in knots over something that was really nothing? What a colossal waste of emotional energy.

In an earlier chapter, I told the story of how Bill Bright got down on his knees as a young man, wrote out a contract, and actually signed his life away to Jesus Christ. After putting his signature on that document, he told the Lord, "From this day forward, I am a slave of Jesus Christ."

Now, I'm not saying that Dr. Bright never became concerned or anxious about life as the years went by, because he was human, just like us. But I believe there was a great deal he *might* have worried about, but never did. He had given it all to Christ and wasn't worried about that which did not belong to him. Instead, he poured his mental and emotional energy into reaching the world for Jesus Christ. What a wonderful way to live.

At age twenty, I made a traumatic discovery. I was in my college apartment, studying for a test, when I scratched my head and a couple of hairs fell out. I thought that was strange, so I scratched again and another few hairs fell out. I scratched a third time, and more fell out. I stopped scratching . . . and started crying. Oh no! Not me! Yes, me. My thick, wonderful hair was going to bite the dust, and bite it at a young age.

Over the next seven years, I started losing more and more hair. I agonized the loss. I spent untold hours in the bathroom, carefully combing my remaining locks and lying to myself that I hadn't really lost that much . . . and that the losing had stopped. But I would snap back to reality whenever I saw an old friend from high school or college who, invariably, would stare at my receding, thinning hairline. Obviously, the process had not stopped.

> *If you will lose all your possessions to the Lord, you will quit worrying about them. It is just that wonderfully simple!*

Well, one day I made a decision. Shave it all off. Go Mr. Clean. And when I did . . . the difficulty was over. I wasn't losing any more. I wasn't experiencing old friends staring at my ever-changing, ever-thinning hairline. I was now totally bald. And I was totally free.

Here is the point: The toughest part of losing your hair is going through the losing process. But once you lose it, completely lose it, you aren't concerned about it anymore. I always look the same. My part is not changing month by month as my hair thins. There is now nothing left to part!

What is true of my hair is also true of your possessions. If you will lose them all to the Lord, you will quit worrying about them. It is just that wonderfully simple!

THE BEST CURE

The best cure for worry you and I could ever embrace would be to tell the Lord, "It's all Yours. My health, *Yours*. My finances, *Yours*.

My wife, *Yours*. My kids, *Yours*. My career, my reputation, my future? *Yours, Yours, Yours*." Then, once you "lose" it all, there is no longer any fear of anticipated loss. Why? Because it's already gone!

One day someone ran up to John Wesley, founder of the Methodist Church, with this distressing news, "John, your house has burned to the ground."

"That's impossible!" replied Wesley.

"John, we saw it with our own eyes. Your house is gone!"

"That's impossible. You see, I don't own a house. God gave me a place to live in. I only manage that house for Him. If He didn't put the fire out, that's His problem. He'll have to put me somewhere else."[7]

Wesley had the right perspective. Give over the ownership of all that you possess to God, and you won't have to worry about it.

PART THREE: SEEK GOD FIRST IN YOUR LIFE

"But seek first His kingdom and His righteousness, and all these things will be added to you."

MATTHEW 6:33

This is the final part of the three-part action plan. Seek God first!

It's one thing to write about signing your life and your possessions over to the Lord, but we all know it's easier said than done. How are we to do it? How can we actually turn everything over to the Lord, and then live in light of that decision?

The answer is by seeking God every day.

The Message translation paraphrases Matthew 6:33–34 this way: "Steep your life in God-reality, God-initiative, God-provisions.

Don't worry about missing out. You'll find all your everyday human concerns will be met. Give your entire attention to what God is doing right now, and don't get worked up about what may or may not happen tomorrow. God will help you deal with whatever hard things come up when the time comes."

Seek God every single day. Seek His kingdom and His purposes every single day. And don't seek Him second, third, fourth, or tenth. Seek Him *first*. Come before Him every morning and reaffirm your contract with Him: "Lord, everything in my life belongs to You."

This is truly the best and most peaceful way to live. It's also a *supernatural* way to live. It goes against the grain of our flesh, the strong pull of our culture, and our own human logic. The fact is, we won't be able to give Him ownership of everything every day unless we seek Him every day.

The psalmist said, "Seek the LORD and His strength; seek His face continually" (Ps. 105:4). Notice that word, *continually*. That's the literal meaning behind the phrase translated "seek first" in Matthew 6:33. Seek Him continually. Don't stop. Don't turn back. Don't get distracted. Pursue Him all the time, but serve Him one day at a time. Matthew 6:34 says, "Do not worry about tomorrow; for tomorrow will care for itself. Each day has enough trouble of its own."

Worry is rooted in what's going to happen or what might happen. We're really not worried about what has already happened. We may celebrate the past, regret the past, or even grieve about it, but we don't worry over it. Worry, as we have said, is the anticipated loss—whether real or imaginary—of a valued possession. Given that definition, worry always looks to the future, and it looks with a negative frown. Quit living in the worries of the future and start living in the joys of today!

ONE DAY AT A TIME

No matter how many days God gives us, He gives them to us one day at a time. So when you think about it . . . today is all we have.

That may sound like a cliché, but it's one of the most basic principles in all of life. Yesterday is gone, and tomorrow may never come. All you really have is today. "How do you know what is going to happen tomorrow?" the apostle James asked. "For the length of your lives is as uncertain as the morning fog—now you see it; soon it is gone" (James 4:14 TLB).

In the Lord's model prayer that He gave us—the one we call "the Lord's Prayer"—He tells us that we are to pray, "Give us this day our daily bread" (Matt. 6:11). Not tomorrow's bread or next week's bread. God is a daily provider who provides for our needs *today*.

It was the same way in the Old Testament with the manna He provided for the children of Israel in the wilderness. It was called "the bread of angels," and it was a sweet, sustaining food that was easy to gather and loaded with all the necessary vitamins and minerals. Through Moses, God instructed them to gather it every morning. He further warned them not to attempt to hoard it or store it overnight in any way. If they did, the stored manna would breed worms. They were to gather only as much as they would use on any given day.

As you might imagine, some of the people paid no attention to that restriction, and tried to store it away "for a rainy day." Doubtless, they said to themselves, "Okay, I'll gather Monday's food—but maybe I should get enough for Tuesday and Wednesday, too. After all, what if God *doesn't* show up with manna tomorrow? When it comes to

God is a daily provider. We are to trust Him one day at a time and not become anxious over what we may require tomorrow.

food and survival, you can never be too careful." (Yes, but you can be too faithless.)

Lo and behold, when the disobedient Israelites looked at their stored manna on Tuesday, it was horrible, rotten, and full of worms . . . just like God had said it would be.

What is the lesson here? God is a *daily* provider. He provides for Monday's needs on Monday, and Tuesday's needs on Tuesday. We are to trust Him one day at a time and not become anxious over what we may require tomorrow. He will be there tomorrow, too, with more than enough grace to help you in your time of need. But He does not provide tomorrow's grace today. He only gives grace for today's issues.

One day, when my middle daughter, Amy, was in the third grade, she forgot her lunch. She called me at 9:00 a.m. to tell me to bring her lunch. I said, "No problem. I'm on it. When is your lunch period?" She told me noon, and I was good to go.

I arrived at her school at 11:55, lunch in hand, and I was seated in the cafeteria, waiting for her to come in with her class. When she arrived, she was visibly upset. I said, "Amy, what's wrong?" She replied, "Dad, I thought you were going to bring me my lunch. I have been worried all morning because you did not come even though I called you."

"Hmmm," I said. "When is your lunch period?"

"Twelve o'clock," she responded.

"And what time is it now?"

"It's twelve o'clock."

"Okay, here's your lunch." And I handed over the lunch bag.

She looked at me with bewilderment but realized she had been worrying needlessly. Her dad came through just like he promised, at just the right time.

Don't we tend to be a lot like Amy? We ask God for things we need . . . and then freak out with worry because it is 10:00 a.m. and He hasn't delivered our *lunch* yet. But God's response is simply, *"I haven't delivered it yet because you don't need it yet. Trust Me and quit worrying! Your* lunch *will be there when the clock strikes twelve, because that is when you need it."*

Never forget, God is a daily, on-time provider.

ENTHRONE HIM AS YOUR ONE AND ONLY MASTER

In my Bible, the heading for verses 25–34 of Matthew 6 says: "The Cure for Anxiety." I think the editors of that study Bible should have backed that heading up one verse. Verse 24 fits right in with the Lord's whole argument: "No one can serve two masters; for either he will hate the one and love the other, or he will be devoted to the one and despise the other. You cannot serve God and wealth."

In this statement, the Lord is speaking of a very simple and basic test. Are you anxious about your life? Are you worried about tomorrow? Are you tied in knots thinking about your investments and all your stuff? If you are, then you're serving the wrong master. You're serving the god of money, stuff, and material possessions.

If you are anxious about your life, it reveals that you're serving the wrong master.

How can you tell if the Lord Jesus Christ is really your God, and if He's really enthroned as God in your heart? *It's when you aren't worried about all the "things" in your life.* Jesus is the Prince of Peace, and when He truly takes the throne as Sovereign and Lord in your heart, you will have His peace. You won't be uptight and distracted, worried about what might happen sometime down the road. You won't find yourself getting tossed about like a shoe in a dog's mouth, being stretched and pulled back and forth. That's not happening in you. Why? Because you're totally at peace, resting in the Prince of Peace Himself.

Yet, there have been many wonderful, sweet people who love God but have become caught up with multiple worries. One of the Lord's best earthly friends, Martha of Bethany, was such a person. And one day Jesus had to speak to her about that, eyeball to eyeball, soul to soul.

She and her sister, Mary, were hosting the Lord and His disciples for a meal in their home, and Martha had begun to flip out over all that had to be done . . . and Mary was not helping! Martha told the Lord how frustrated she was—and what He needed to do about it to make it right. Sweetly and gently, the Lord said to her, "Martha, Martha, you are worried and bothered about so many things; but only one thing is necessary, for Mary has chosen the good part, which shall not be taken away from her" (Luke 10:41–42). Mary, caught up with being in the presence of Jesus and hearing His words, was at His feet in perfect peace. She had enthroned the Prince of Peace in her heart and wasn't worried about a thing. Jesus wanted that same peace for Martha . . . and He wants it for you too.

WHAT ABOUT YOU?

Are you "worried and bothered about so many things"? Is the smoke alarm of anxiety blaring in your soul today? The time to silence that annoying alarm is now. You *can* experience the Lord's perfect peace as you put this threefold action plan from Matthew 6 into practice: (1) trust God to take care of you; (2) give God ownership of all that you possess; and (3) seek God first in your life.

Try it and see for yourself. It is the Lord's proven cure when anxiety attacks.

FIVE

ANGER

The Beast Within

He who is slow to anger is better than the mighty, and he who rules his spirit, than he who captures a city.

PROVERBS 16:32

I know, LORD, that we humans are not in control of our own lives.

JEREMIAH 10:23 CEV

If you're breathing and have a pulse, you will find yourself dealing with a flash of anger from time to time. It comes with the territory of being an imperfect human being born in a broken world.

There are some people, however, who simply *live* angry. They breathe anger in and out, like oxygen and carbon dioxide. It seems as though they're mad about something all the time.

At this moment, you may be saying to yourself, "This chapter is definitely for someone else. He's not writing about me. I don't have an anger problem at all."

Just for fun, then, let's take a little anger test to see how you do. Ready?

- Do minor irritations cause you to lose your cool? You're out for dinner and you spill food down the front of your clothing. Let's say . . . a big splatter of red salsa on a clean white shirt. Does that drive you crazy? You get up in the middle of the night and stub your toe. Do you freak out? Just a little? You're at your computer and about to hit F10 to save your document—but the hard drive crashes *before* you have a chance to save all your work. Do you just want to slam your fist through the monitor?

- Do you tend to be in conflict often? Do you always seem to be in some kind of dispute or fight with this person or that? Maybe you've found yourself thinking, *I can't get along at home, I can't get along at school, and I can't seem to get along at work. What's wrong with everybody? I don't know how it happens, but I always seem to end up with all these disagreeable, argumentative, unreasonable people in my life!* Hmmm.

- Do you blame others for your outbursts? "She *made* me angry." "He said such and such to me, and that just pushed my buttons." "It's his fault I lost my temper."

- Do you have trouble submitting to authority? Do you just hate it when you have to submit to the boss? Do you grit your teeth when that teacher or coach takes you to task over something? Do you find it difficult to yield to the authority of the church (or your pastor) when you feel as if you know better on a given issue?

- Do you have trouble forgiving people who have hurt you in the past? When you're reminded of certain people who have wronged you, do you feel the anger welling up inside you all over again?

- Do you "lose it" in traffic? Isn't it interesting how driving on a congested highway can expose anger issues in no time? Does it expose any in you? Do you find yourself wanting to retaliate against rude, foolish, or preoccupied drivers who cut you off, ride on your tail, space out when the light turns green, or slow you down to a crawl? (Comic George Carlin used to quip, "Have you ever noticed that anybody driving slower than you is an idiot, and anyone going faster than you is a maniac?"[1] How true!)

We could all cite situations that have caused us (temporarily) to lose our cool. But what happens when you find yourself becoming unreasonably angry over small things? Why do people sometimes fly into a rage over the seemingly insignificant words or actions of others? To answer those questions, we have to look deeper than the situations that make us angry to the real *source* of our anger.

What Causes the Anger?

Why do we get angry? What do flashes of over-the-top anger tell you? (Note: In this chapter, I am not talking about "righteous indignation" over sin and social injustice. That type of anger is good and godly. This discussion focuses on *unrighteous* anger that causes serious problems in life and relationships.)

I believe the smoke alarm of anger communicates this important message: Warning! Your God-given desire for control is on fire.

EMOTION: Anger
WARNING: Your God-given desire for control is on fire.

When you really stop and think about it, most of our anger finds its roots in our desire to somehow control the people and the environment around us. In other words, we want things to go the way *we* want them to go. If you don't believe me, consider this: Why do so many of us get so angry watching our favorite football team lose? Because we wanted them to win! We didn't want them to throw an interception in the end zone in the closing seconds of the game, when a touchdown would have sealed the victory. That's *not* what we wanted. So our team loses . . . and we lose it!

Every time you and I get angry, it's because something happened to us that we didn't want to happen. Am I right? And the thinking behind that anger goes like this: *I deserve better!* I deserve a computer that works right. I deserve clear traffic when I'm on the road. I deserve my favorite team's wide receiver to catch the ball in the end zone. I deserve a winning team.

Mark it down—when anger strikes, the smoke alarm blares out, "I deserve better than this!"

MADE IN HIS IMAGE

God created humanity in His own image. Genesis 1:26 makes that crystal clear: "Then God said, 'Let Us make man in Our image, according to Our likeness, and let them rule over the fish of the sea and over the birds of the sky and over the cattle and over all the earth, and over every creeping thing that creeps on the earth.'" Within the image of God, there is authority, responsibility, and control. Since we are made in His image, we have a hardwired desire to exercise some degree of control over our environment.

When God formed Adam and Eve, He made them perfect, and then He said to them, "Be fruitful and multiply, and fill the earth, and subdue it" (Gen. 1:28). That was their job. They were to take dominion over creation and rule over it as vice-regents under God.

But then, in Genesis 3, Adam and Eve fell into sin. They disobeyed God's one and only prohibition by eating of the tree God had commanded them not to eat. When they fell, their God-given desire for authority and control became twisted and polluted. Now, instead of having a God-consciousness and a God-focus, Adam and Eve had a *self*-consciousness and a *self*-focus.

And then control became all about *me*. Life became all about *me*.

I think that's one of the big keys to understanding where our anger originates. God created us with a desire to exercise control, but that good and legitimate desire has become warped and distorted by sin. As a result, we want to control things—events, situations, and people—in accordance with our selfish desires and for our selfish ends. We want things to go the way we want them to go! When they don't—when our desires are frustrated—we're seized with anger.

God created us with a desire to exercise control, but that good and legitimate desire has become warped and distorted by sin.

Have you noticed this phenomenon of selfish control take hold in your life? I've seen it in my life more times than I like to admit. It is an inescapable reality brought about by original sin.

How Can You Silence the Alarm?

Maybe you're in a season of life where you feel angry all the time, where the least little thing will set you off. You have a hair-trigger temper, and if somebody crosses you, you blow up like a volcano.

Nobody really wants to live this way. Nobody actually enjoys having a heart filled with anger, resentment, and bitterness. It's a terrible way to live. And you can also be sure of this: nobody likes to be *around* anyone like that, either.

Perhaps you grew up with a dad who was a walking time bomb. You always had to tiptoe around the house on eggshells for fear of setting him off. Or your wife or husband flies into a rage over seemingly trivial offenses or frustrations. Or perhaps it is an angry child who continually teeters on the edge of ballistic. It's definitely not fun for those who have to live under the same roof with an angry person.

So what do you do to silence the alarm? How do you deal with the issue of always wanting control? That's what we'll be exploring in this chapter as we look at the life of an angry prophet named Jonah.

THE STORY OF JONAH: A LESSON IN ANGER

The word of the LORD came to Jonah the son of Amittai saying, "Arise, go to Nineveh the great city and cry against it, for their wickedness has come up before Me."

JONAH 1:1–2

When God's call came to Jonah, it was crystal clear. There could be no mistaking the who, what, when, where, or why. The prophet Jonah understood the Lord's command all too clearly, and took immediate action: "But Jonah rose up to flee to Tarshish from the presence of the LORD" (v. 3).

Did you catch that? Jonah heard what God had said—then went in the *opposite* direction. That's not what you'd call a great launch into a new ministry. When the call came to go east to Nineveh, Jonah hightailed it to the port of Joppa to board a ship headed for Tarshish, the western edge of the known world. This was no accident or misunderstanding. There was no mix-up with the prophet's itinerary or e-tickets. He didn't board the wrong ship by mistake. Jonah was deliberately running away from God, far away . . . as if that were even possible!

Did he really imagine God would let him get away with that? Let's pick up the fast-moving narrative from Scripture:

The LORD hurled a great wind on the sea and there was a great storm on the sea so that the ship was about to break up. Then the sailors became afraid and every man cried to his god, and they threw the cargo which was in the ship into the sea to lighten it for them. But Jonah had gone below into the hold of the ship, lain down and fallen sound asleep. So the captain approached him and said, "How is it that you are sleeping? Get up; call on your god. Perhaps your god will be concerned about us so that we will not perish."

Each man said to his mate, "Come, let us cast lots so we may learn on whose account this calamity has struck us." So they cast lots and the lot fell on Jonah. Then they said to him, "Tell us, now! On whose account has this calamity struck us? What is your occupation? And where do you come from? What is your country? From what people are you?" He said to them, "I am a Hebrew, and I fear the LORD God of heaven who made the sea and the dry land."

Then the men became extremely frightened and they said to him, "How could you do this?" For the men knew that he was fleeing from the presence of the LORD, because he had told them. So they said to him, "What should we do to you that the sea may become calm for us?"—for the sea was becoming increasingly stormy. He said to them, "Pick me up and throw me into the sea. Then the sea will become calm for you, for I know that on account of me this great storm has come upon you." (vv. 4–12)

The sailors were a little reluctant to toss the rebellious prophet over the side—at least at first. But the more they delayed, the worse the storm became. In the end, they probably looked at one another and said, "We have no other option. What do we have to lose?" So they took the Hebrew prophet at his word and pitched him into the angry, raging sea.

Just that quickly, the storm was over.

In the meantime, God prepared a great fish to swallow Jonah. And in the belly of that fish, amid the harmful effects and foul stench of stomach acid, Jonah got his heart right with God. As a result, he was given a taxi ride to dry land.

And then comes one of my favorite verses in the Bible: "Now the word of the LORD came to Jonah the second time" (Jonah 3:1).

And then comes one of my favorite verses in the Bible: "Now the word of the LORD came to Jonah the second time" (Jonah 3:1). God is the God of second chances.

Why do I love this seemingly simple verse so much? Because God was gracious to His disobedient servant, and He gave him another opportunity to obey. And that's exactly what He has done for me in my life, time after time after time. God is the God of second chances, third chances, and three-hundredth chances. He is *the God of all grace* (1 Peter 5:10). He is unfathomably rich in mercy. Aren't you glad for that?

But God's great mercy doesn't mean we will dodge all the natural outcomes or consequences of our sin and stubbornness. Jonah had to have a "time-out" in the belly of the fish. Trust me when I tell you he came out of that fish much worse for wear. Yes, he got right with God, but he felt the physical effects of his rebellion. Remember, Jonah was not Pinocchio. His body suffered in that underwater prison.

Back on dry land, Jonah heard the voice of the Lord once again. God said: "Arise, go to Nineveh the great city and proclaim to it the proclamation which I am going to tell you" (Jonah 3:2). And this time, Jonah followed the Lord's instructions to a T. And this was the message God wanted proclaimed from one end of the city to the other: "Yet forty days and Nineveh will be overthrown" (v. 4).

But what happened next? For whatever reason (and wouldn't you just know it), those cruel, hard-hearted, wicked Assyrians who lived in Nineveh simply *melted* at this message of impending judgment from the Lord. From the king on down, they believed God's Word and repented. They put on sackcloth. They sat in ashes. They fasted. They prayed. They cried out to God for mercy.

What did God do? He saw their change of heart, heard their prayers, and mercifully aborted Operation Destroy Nineveh.

And what did Jonah, God's spokesman, think of all that? Surely he rejoiced with God over their response. Surely he exclaimed, "Praise the Lord!" when the destruction of the city was canceled, right? Wrong! He was so angry he was spitting nails.

> But it greatly displeased Jonah and he became angry. He prayed to the LORD and said, "Please LORD, was not this what I said while I was still in my own country? Therefore in order to forestall this I fled to Tarshish, for I knew that You are a gracious and compassionate God, slow to anger and abundant in lovingkindness, and one who relents concerning calamity. Therefore now, O LORD, please take my life from me, for death is better to me than life. (4:1–3)

God had been angry at the Assyrians and their capital city of Nineveh because of their great wickedness, merciless cruelty, and all the horrifying atrocities they committed against their defeated foes. But then, when those same despicable people genuinely responded to God's message and turned to Him in repentance, God forgave them.

Jonah hated that. And he was angry all the way to the bone.

Jonah 4:1 says, "It greatly displeased Jonah." The Hebrew term translated "greatly" could also be translated "highly," "violently," or "exceedingly." In other words, he was filled to the brim with displeasure.

Here is how *The Message* renders Jonah 4:1–3: "Jonah was furious. He lost his temper. He yelled at GOD, 'GOD! I knew it—when I was back home, I knew this was going to happen! That's why I ran off to Tarshish! I knew you were sheer grace and mercy, not easily angered, rich in love, and ready at the drop of a hat to turn your plans of punishment into a program of forgiveness!'

"Jonah was furious. He lost his temper. He yelled at GOD."
(Jonah 4:1 MSG)

"'So, GOD, if you won't kill them, kill *me*! I'm better off dead!'"

(Can you imagine blowing up at God like that?)

When Scripture says Jonah was *angry*, the Hebrew term literally means he "became hot, having burning anger." And with whom was he so furious? He was angry with God. "I knew this was going to happen!" he raged. "I knew You were a gracious and compassionate God, slow to anger and abundant in lovingkindness."

And that's a *bad* thing?

Obviously, Jonah thought it was a bad thing when that lovingkindness and compassion were extended to the Assyrians. You see, Jonah was like the rest of the Israelites in his hatred for the Assyrians, the arrogant, evil, unbelievably cruel enemies of Israel. The prophets Amos and Hosea had prophesied that Assyria would come one day and destroy Israel, which is exactly what they did in 722 BC. God forbid that any Israel-loving prophet should ever help the Assyrians, Israel's future destroyers. So Jonah was saying, "I hate these miserable Assyrians. They're the worst of the worst. They don't deserve one thin shred of mercy or grace. Like a cancerous tumor in the body, they deserve to be excised and eradicated from the earth." God's decision to forgive and hold off judgment on the Ninevites may have also stung Jonah's pride. He had faithfully preached the message, "Yet forty days and Nineveh will be overthrown!" But then God changed His mind. He didn't overthrow Nineveh in forty days. In fact, He didn't overthrow Nineveh for another 130 years.

So where did that leave Jonah? With egg on his face, as far as he was concerned. "Well, thanks a lot, God. You've made a false prophet out of me! I said You were going to destroy them, and now You've changed Your mind. So that makes me a fraud. And what are people going to say when I go back to Israel? 'Where have you been, Jonah? Leading a revival in Assyria? Helping our enemies, the Assyrians? Are you insane? You're nothing more than a traitor and a worthless turncoat.'

"My reputation is trashed, Lord. I'm just so angry that I'd rather die!"

Jonah was angry because things didn't go the way he had expected and hoped. God didn't do what Jonah had longed for Him to do— which was to fry the city of Nineveh.

The smoke alarm in Jonah's life was going off like an air-raid siren. In fact, we can still hear it thousands of years later.

This very book of Jonah, however, teaches us two essentials that we must do if we're going to silence the shrilling smoke alarm of anger in our lives.

First Essential: Recognize That God Is in Control

Jonah was angry because things didn't go the way he had expected and hoped. God didn't do what Jonah had longed for Him to do—which was to fry the city of Nineveh with a few well-placed lightning bolts or a volcanic eruption under the king's palace. Jonah may have even thought, *God, if I had been You, I would have gone back to the Sodom and Gomorrah playbook and rained fire and brimstone on those wicked pagans. I would have nuked every last one of them and turned the capital city of Nineveh into a pile of rubble.*

This unhappy, disgruntled prophet wasn't willing to see that *God* was in control of all these things, not Jonah. He was angry because he wanted to control the situation and wanted it to go his way. After all, he felt his way was right and God's was wrong in this matter.

But how true is this line of thinking? How realistic is it to expect that things will always go the way we want them to, and that we will somehow maintain control over our own lives? It's not realistic at all! There's so *much* we can't control. We can't control traffic. We can't control weather. We have trouble controlling our own children, so much of the time.

You know who controls everything? God! Scripture calls Him "He who is the blessed and only Sovereign, the King of kings and Lord of lords" (1 Tim. 6:15). God is the Supreme Ruler—the One in charge of it all. He says in Isaiah 45:18, "I am the Lord, and there is no other; besides Me there is no God."

Jeremiah came to that conclusion early in his ministry, admitting to the Lord (and to himself), "I know, O Lord, that a man's way is not in himself, nor is it in a man who walks to direct his steps" (Jer. 10:23).

Furthermore, the Lord has no need of counselors. He doesn't need to consult a board or the stockholders to see if He can get His plan ratified. Neither does He take a poll or put His decisions up for a vote. God is the great King, and He certainly didn't have to check with Jonah before deciding to offer mercy toward the Ninevites.

God consults no one, and He calls all the shots.

Anchor this important truth in your heart: God consults no one, and He calls all the shots.

In Matthew 10:29, the Lord Jesus asked, "Are not two little sparrows sold for a penny? And yet not one of them will fall to the ground without your Father's leave [consent] and notice" (AMP).

Who was in control in the book of Jonah? Just run your eyes over the text, and you'll immediately see the answer (emphasis added):

> "*The Lord hurled* a great wind on the sea." (1:4)
>
> "*The Lord appointed* a great fish to swallow Jonah." (1:17)
>
> "*The Lord commanded* the fish, and it vomited Jonah up onto the dry land." (2:10)
>
> "*The Lord God appointed* a plant and it grew up over Jonah." (4:6)
>
> "*God appointed* a worm when dawn came . . . and it attacked the plant." (4:7)
>
> "*God appointed* a scorching east wind. . . ." (4:8)

God is in control of everything. He controls the wind, the weather, the sea, the fish, the plants, the worms. He is over the big things (winds and waves), the little things (worms and plants), and everything in between. As Psalm 135:6 tells us, "Whatever the LORD pleases, He does, in heaven and in earth, in the seas and in all deeps."

Not long ago, I heard about three behind-the-plate baseball umpires who got into a conversation at a get-together. The first one said, "Some of those pitches are balls, and some are strikes, and I call 'em as I see 'em."

The second umpire was more confident, asserting, "Some of 'em are balls and some of 'em are strikes, but I call 'em as they *are*."

The third umpire, however, one-upped them both, saying, "Some of 'em are balls and some of 'em are strikes, but they ain't nothing until I call 'em!"

Now, there's an umpire who is in control, or at least *thinks* he is.

You and I may desire control in certain situations; we may long for control with all our hearts, and we may even imagine we have some measure of control. But it isn't true. It's mostly illusion. We really control only one thing in life—how we will respond to God— but God controls everything.

DOES IT MAKE SENSE?

Does everything God does make sense to us? Of course not! In fact, most of what the Lord does makes little sense to us. His infinite, divine ways don't line up with finite, human logic. In Isaiah 55, God clearly tells us this is the case:

> "For My thoughts are not your thoughts,
> Nor are your ways My ways," declares the Lord.
> "For as the heavens are higher than the earth,
> So are My ways higher than your ways
> And My thoughts than your thoughts." (vv. 8–9)

Do you think it made sense to Abram when God told him to leave his homeland and go to a land he had never seen and would never own in his lifetime? Did it make sense to Job when God allowed him to lose all of his possessions and his seven sons and three daughters in a single day? Do you think it seemed right to Joseph when God just looked on with seeming indifference as he was thrown into a pit by his own brothers, sold into slavery in Egypt, accused of a crime he never committed, and locked up for years in a dark, slimy dungeon? Did it seem sensible to Habakkuk that God would use a nation more evil and violent than his own as an instrument of discipline on His people?

The lesson is simple: You are not in control; God is.

None of those things make logical sense to us. Neither did it make sense to the believers in the Jerusalem church when God allowed Stephen, that great man of God just beginning a dynamic ministry for Jesus Christ, to be arrested, tried, and stoned to death by a hateful mob of religious people. But He did.

OUT OF OUR CONTROL

Have you ever noticed how we so often find ourselves blindsided by difficulties, setbacks, and tragedies that strike us like bolts of lightning out of the blue? Why does that happen? What is the lesson? The lesson is simple: *You are not in control; God is.*

My friend Laura went to the doctor for a routine test, and when the results came back, the doctor told her, "You have colon cancer, and it's stage III." Just that suddenly—on what had been an otherwise "normal" day—she found herself looking at extended chemo treatments, surgery, and a temporary colostomy. In that moment, she realized that life might never be "normal" again.

Maybe you've received one of those life-altering phone calls telling you that one of your family members has been killed in a car wreck. One moment your loved one was healthy, strong, full of plans and dreams and laughter, and the next moment, he or she is gone. *Bam!* It happens that quickly. Life really does turn on a dime.

Just recently, I heard about a woman in her early fifties who was hiking with her husband near Mount Rainier in Washington State. After a delicious breakfast at a mountain lodge, the two of them walked through late-summer wildflowers and stood in awe at the beauty of Rainier's mighty, snow-crowned peak. But then, on the way back to the car, her husband simply collapsed at her feet and died from an aneurism.

The woman returned to her house that night alone, torn from her husband and best friend.

God, however, rarely answers our whys. As a wise friend once told me, "God is not in the business of explaining; He is in the business of sustaining."

Our natural tendency, of course, is to ask why. "God, why did this happen? Why in the world would You let something like this crash into my life?"

God, however, rarely answers our whys. As a wise friend once told me, "God is not in the business of explaining; He is in the business of sustaining."

Make no mistake about it: In our disappointment and grief, we will naturally cry out to God, "Why did this happen? Why did I lose my job? Why did my loved one die? Why did I get sick? Why did my parents divorce? Why, why, why?" And this is normal, natural, and human. But what is God's answer to our "Why?"

"Trust Me."

I was very blessed to have a wonderful father-in-law, named

Gerald Canon. He was a strong preacher and a caring pastor. His church members loved him dearly.

When he was in his early sixties, he suffered a massive stroke. It came without warning and brought tremendous upheaval to his life and family. For weeks on end, we didn't know whether he would live or die. He was hospitalized for months. We couldn't even communicate with him because he was so incapacitated.

Finally, after many weeks in a somewhat comatose state, he was able to talk with us again. I remember standing by his bedside and asking him, "Gerald, what is God telling you through all of this? What is He speaking to your heart?"

Gerald could have been angry. Instead of caring about anything God might be saying through his trial, he could have launched into a tirade against the God who had seemingly abandoned him and allowed him to experience such tremendous pain and loss. But instead, he looked up at me and simply responded with these two words, "Trust Me!" God was saying to him what He says to all of us in times of tragedy and hardship and those devastating "Why!?" moments: *"My child, will you just trust Me?"*

We may not always like that answer, but I can't think of a better one this side of heaven. *Trust Me.*

But Back to Jonah . . .

In Jonah's disappointment and anger, the Lord came to him and said, in effect, *"Do you have good reason to be angry? You need to trust Me. I'm in control."* The fact is, the Lord never makes a mistake. You'll never hear the word "Oops!" coming from the throne room of heaven. God knows the end from the beginning, and everything in between. And He is good. He does all things well. He is worthy of our complete and total trust.

In Ezekiel 18, the exiled Jews in Babylon were angry at the Lord because things weren't turning out the way they wanted them to. They were saying, in essence, "We deserve better than this," and "The way of the Lord is not right."

The Lord replied with these words: "You say, 'The way of the Lord is not right.' Hear now, O house of Israel! Is My way not right? Is it not your ways that are not right?" (v. 25).

But here's what we do. We, the finite, fallible creatures that we are, come before our infinite, infallible God and demand answers and explanations for His actions, which we just *know* are wrong in this given instance. Hmmm. We *know* the infinite, perfect, all-knowing God is wrong, and we, the finite, flawed, very-little-knowing people are right?

How foolish we are to think we know better than God.

How foolish we are to think we know better than God. It's like bringing a little teacup to the Pacific Ocean, erroneously believing the cup has the capacity to understand and contain the depth and breadth of the vast sea. Can you imagine that little teacup having the audacity to say to the mighty Pacific Ocean, "Hey, I know that you're not right because I am filled up to my tiny little rim with knowledge and understanding." And the Pacific Ocean roars back, "I am filled with zillions upon zillions upon zillions of teacups. I believe I understand things much better than you do, so why don't you just trust me to do what's best?"

Paul wrote in Romans 11:33, "Oh, the depth of the riches both of the wisdom and knowledge of God! How unsearchable are His judgments and unfathomable His ways!" God is our Pacific Ocean. When we don't understand, we would be wise to trust that He does.

One day, in the bright morning light of eternity, we will begin to understand why He did what He did (if it still matters to us). On this side of heaven, however, we receive small glimpses of greater realities . . . as much as we can handle. The Bible says, "Now we know in part. . . . Now we see in a mirror dimly" (1 Cor. 13:9, 12), but in His presence we'll see everything clearly. And when we stand before Him, when we see life from His perspective, we will say, "Lord, You did all things well! You did every single thing in my life perfectly, Lord, and I'm so glad. Thank You, Lord."

He never makes a mistake.

Again, then, the first essential in dealing with the root cause of anger is *recognizing that God is in control.* No one could have wronged you had God not *allowed* it. That thief couldn't have stolen from you, and your former friend couldn't have spread lies about you unless God allowed it. Not even a sparrow falls to the earth without God's permission. And God has a wonderful plan for each undesired situation, even if He hasn't yet shared that plan with you.

SECOND ESSENTIAL: CHOOSE GOD'S GRACE OVER YOUR CONTROL

When God chose to save Nineveh instead of destroying it, Jonah was so gripped by burning, boiling anger that he asked God to kill him on the spot. You can almost hear him whine, "LORD, my life is ruined! My reputation is trashed. You're not going to follow through with what You had me preach. You're not doing it right! So just snuff me out, okay? I don't want to keep on living. I don't want to go home looking like a fool. So stick a fork in me, because I'm done, and I just want to die."

Jonah was sick with disappointment and seething with rage. Yet the Lord dealt so sweetly and patiently with His servant. "Do you have good reason to be angry?" He asked the prophet (v. 4).

I think if I had been God, I may have been a bit more impatient with Jonah at this point. The prophet had already disobeyed and fled from the Lord's command. Then God saved his life by having a great fish swallow him and deliver him safely to land again. Jonah finally obeyed, but he then became so angry at the Lord that he wouldn't even give Him the courtesy of an answer to His question. Instead, the prophet turned away in a huff, left the city, and sat under a little homemade shelter, waiting to see what would happen.

If I had been God, I believe I would have said in response to Jonah's prayer, "So you want Me to kill you, Jonah? Request granted. You're dead."

If I had been God, I believe I would have said, "So, you want Me to kill you, Jonah? Request granted. You're dead. I'm sick and tired of your disobedience and disrespectful, ignorant rants." (We can all be glad that I am not God.)

God, however, was gentle and patient with His unhappy, sulking servant, just as He was with angry Cain in Genesis 4. There, the Lord offers great insight into anger. "Why are you angry?" He asked Cain. "And why has your countenance fallen? If you do well, will not your countenance be lifted up? And if you do not do well, sin is crouching at the door; and its desire is for you, but you must master it" (vv. 6–7).

In both cases, when His servants were angry, God asked them *why*. He didn't ask for the sake of His own enlightenment, but for theirs. He was inviting them to really think through their anger and to see just how foolish they were for being angry in the first place. He invites us to do the same.

When we get angry, God gives us both a warning and a way out. *"Be careful here,"* He says. *"If you don't get the right perspective on this destructive emotion, you are liable to do something that has grave consequences. Don't open that door to the actions of your anger because you won't like what is on the other side. Instead, do what is right."*

Perhaps you are dealing with some anger even as you read these words. Maybe you're mad at your employer, the church, your ex, or your parents. Maybe you were physically or emotionally abused by your father, and you've carried anger in your heart toward him for years. What do you do to rid your heart of all that poison?

God's advice to Cain is just as wise for you and me when we're in the grip of anger and bitterness. He said, *"Master the sin crouching at the door by doing what is right."*

So . . . how do we do that?

1. Humble yourself before God.

God is opposed to the proud, but gives grace to the humble. Humble yourselves, therefore, under the mighty hand of God.

1 Peter 5:5–6

Neither Jonah nor Cain humbled himself before God. As a result, neither were able to rightly process their anger. Angry Cain opened the door to the sin that was crouching behind it, and he went out and murdered his brother. Ticked-off Jonah was left pouting and miserable on the eastern outskirts of Nineveh. News flash:

until you and I choose to humble ourselves before the almighty God, we won't do any better with our anger.

Neither Jonah nor Cain humbled himself before God. As a result, neither were able to rightly process their anger.

God gives grace—His unmerited favor and power—to those who willingly humble themselves before Him. Remember, *He* is in control, not *you*. He sits on the throne of the universe, not you. He calls the shots, not you. He is the Pacific Ocean, and you're just a teacup . . . so clear your angry head, look up and see the King, and humble yourself before Him.

God has a "mighty hand" (1Pet. 5:6). He knows all, sees all, and rules over all. So if we want His help in our moments of fury, we need to honestly pray a prayer like this: "Lord, this situation really stinks. It makes no sense to me what You are doing right now. I am so mad about this, and I think what is happening is so wrong . . . but as an act of my will, I yield right now to You. You are God, and I'm just lowly me. I choose to humble myself and claim Your grace to help me in my time of need."

Guess what? If you will do that, God's grace will be there for you in that very moment. You will experience a change within. And your anger will begin to drain away, like air rushing from a punctured tire. If you don't believe me, try it and see.

2. FORGIVE THOSE WHO HAVE HURT YOU.

Jonah had a heart full of hate for a whole race of people, an entire nationality. He *despised* the Assyrians. He *loathed* the people who lived in Nineveh. They were Israel's enemies and—in Jonah's mind—God's enemies too. They were idol worshippers, wicked, violent, arrogant, and utterly ruthless. It made no sense to him at all that God would choose to have compassion on them.

Maybe you have a "Ninevite" in your life. You wouldn't use the word "hate," perhaps, but you have a very negative attitude toward that individual. When someone mentions his or her name in conversation, you feel a little lurch in your stomach, and the hair on the back of your neck begins to rise. Those are clear indicators of a Nineveh issue.

Anger usually begins with hurt. Virtually every angry person is a hurting person. Something happened to you that you didn't like, that you didn't want, and it wounded you. If that wound is not dealt with correctly, it will always morph into anger. Always.

Anger usually begins with hurt. Virtually every angry person is a hurting person.

Ephesians 4:26–27 tells us that if we allow the sun to go down on our anger, holding on to that emotion until the next day, we give the devil a "place"—a foothold—in our lives (KJV; NIV). Unresolved anger turns to resentment, which, on the face of it, is a rather passive emotion. It doesn't seem all that toxic or dangerous. But, left unchecked, resentment evolves into bitterness, and if you don't deal with bitterness in your soul, it will soon become out-and-out hatred. It is a deadly anger progression that is unavoidable if unaddressed.

The writer of Hebrews has warned us: "See to it that no one comes short of the grace of God; that no root of bitterness springing up causes trouble, and by it many be defiled" (12:15). Bitterness, then, is clearly a poisonous root that runs underground in the soul, gradually choking out joy, life, and productivity. And not only that, the Bible says that by it, "many are defiled."

Churches are ruined by bitterness. Why? Because bitter people tend to share their dark and tainted views with others. They love to tell you all the negative, harmful things about people they don't like.

And don't kid yourself: people are influenced by this kind of talk. Before long, more people than you may realize will have choked on the bitter water from that poisoned well.

What can you and I do about bitterness? Get rid of it by truly forgiving the person who caused us hurt.

What can you and I do about bitterness? *Get rid of it by truly forgiving the person who caused us hurt.* This is a life-changing action and, when empowered by God's transforming grace, it works like an antivenom shot directly to the heart.

Sometimes I hear people say, "I could *never* forgive her for what she did to me. It's just too much to ask of me to do that." And so, like Jonah and like Cain, they refuse to forgive and refuse to allow God's grace to change their hearts.

BITTERNESS: IT'S LIKE A DIRTY DIAPER

I was never good at changing dirty diapers. Debbie changed many more diapers than I ever did with our three girls. Whether it was a weak stomach and a strong sense of odor, or just a selfish aversion to the task, I had trouble with dirty diapers. When there was no other way out and I had to do it, I'd wrap a towel around my face just to be able to handle the odor. And then, after I got that soiled diaper off the baby, I disposed of it as fast as I could. No one wants to linger in the presence of a dirty diaper.

When it comes to an unforgiving, bitter heart, understand this: Holding on to past hurts is like clinging to a dirty diaper. Refusing to forgive someone who hurt you is just like taking a soiled diaper and, instead of throwing it away, tucking it away in your breast pocket... and carrying it with you everywhere you go. That's exactly what we do when we won't forgive those who have hurt us, whether accidentally or intentionally. We take all that hurt and all that dirt and filth and bring it into our hearts, and we say, "I'm hanging on to this." The irony, of course, is we imagine that by holding on to the dirty diaper, we will somehow hurt the person who has hurt us. How foolish.

Someone once said that unforgiveness is like drinking poison and thinking it will kill the person who hurt you. But it never hurts him; it just hurts you. If *you* drink the poison, then *you* will be poisoned . . . and your offender will go on enjoying his life.

God says you need to forgive, and that's how you get rid of all that anger churning around inside you. You forgive the father who hurt you . . . the child who betrayed you . . . the employer who used and then discarded you . . . the business partner who cheated you . . . the spouse who divorced you . . . the friend who demeaned you. You let it go.

How do you do that? Maybe it will be a little like Peter's experience in Matthew 14, when he crawled over the edge of the boat on that stormy night, and put his foot on the water. He had certainly never walked on water in his whole life until that moment, and really had no idea how he was going to do it this time. But Jesus had said, "Come," so Peter stepped over the edge and did the impossible. And that first step was probably the most frightening one of all.

Even though you may not feel like doing this—even though it may seem as difficult as stepping over the side of a boat on a wild, windswept night—you must say, "God, I need You, and I affirm that at this very moment, I forgive the person who hurt me. Father, You deal with him [or her], and please let Your transforming grace flow through my heart right now."

In Romans 12, Paul wrote: "Never pay back evil with more evil. . . . Do all that you can to live in peace with everyone. Dear friends, never take revenge. Leave that to the righteous anger of God. For the Scriptures say, 'I will take revenge; I will pay them back,' says the LORD" (vv. 17–19 NLT). What if Jonah had followed that advice? What if he had prayed something like this: "Lord, I don't pretend to understand all that You're doing here, but You just go ahead and deal with these Assyrians however You see fit. I'm not going to hate them or dwell on their evil actions. Now, what's my next assignment, Lord? I'm ready to move on." That prayer would have changed his life and ministry.

If you won't forgive those who hurt you, God won't forgive you.

People who refuse to forgive those who have harmed them must deal with the Lord's strong, sobering words in Matthew 6:14–15: "If you forgive others for their transgressions, your heavenly Father will also forgive you. But if you do not forgive others, then your Father will not forgive your transgressions."

Wow. Did you catch that? If you *won't* forgive those who hurt you, He won't forgive you.

Someone once told a famous preacher of yesteryear, "I cannot forgive this man for what he did to me." And that preacher wisely replied, "Well then, I suggest you never sin again, because God won't forgive you if you won't forgive that man."

Maybe that's where you are today. Perhaps you are holding on to a memory of something someone did to you or said to you five years ago—or ten, or twenty, or fifty years ago. You've clung to the dirty diaper of unforgiveness all this time, and it's become toxic to your system. We fool ourselves if we claim that we have a walk with the Lord while still holding on to bitterness and hatred in our hearts. How can you be in fellowship with God when he has told us clearly that He won't forgive our sins unless we forgive the sins of others against us?

When Jonah was in trouble himself, he loved the idea that God was forgiving, gracious, compassionate, and merciful. When he was fighting for his life in the innards of that great fish, he wanted God to show forth those wonderful attributes of kindness and long-suffering toward *him*. But when it came to the people he hated for things they had done to wound him and his nation, he didn't want God to be gracious and merciful. He wanted Him to squash them like a bug. In fact, the prophet was more than willing for a whole city to perish, with no chance for God's mercy, rather than let go of his anger and bitterness.

Be honest here. How much are you like Jonah when it comes to those horrible "Assyrians" in your life? Are you having difficulty forgiving? Then remember how often you have offended God, and how much He has forgiven *you*. You've hurt Him countless times more than anybody could have ever hurt you. You've sinned against God over and over (and over and over . . .) again, and so have I. But God has forgiven us by His grace . . . and that grace enables us to forgive others.

"FORGIVING" GOD?

We've already discussed how ridiculous it is for us to dare to be angry with God. Yet we do it. We get mad because of things that happened that He could have easily prevented: the loved one who died, the marriage that hit the rocks, the child who went astray. So what can we do?

I heard of one pastor who actually told his congregation, "What you need to do to heal emotionally is forgive God." This guy actually encouraged people to *forgive* God, as if God had somehow sinned against them. Inconceivable.

Listen, *no one* ever needs to forgive God, because God has never done anything wrong. He is holy and righteous and perfect in all His ways and in all His dealings with you and me. To be sure, He may have allowed some things to occur in your life that you can't understand, that you can't wrap your mind around, but He has never done anything that requires your forgiveness.

So when we get mad at God, rather than "forgive" Him, we need to come into His presence and tell Him everything that's in our hearts (He knows it anyway) and ask Him to forgive *us*. We need to pray, "Lord, I have been angry at You. Would You please forgive me? Your thoughts are so much higher than my thoughts. I can't begin to see the world and life as You do. And so, God, I come to You, the gracious, compassionate God who knows everything, and ask You to forgive me and change my heart. I don't want to have this bad feeling in my heart toward You." And because God is merciful, He will forgive you. He understands our feelings and our struggles. As David wrote, "He Himself knows our frame; He is mindful that we are but dust" (Ps. 103:14).

MAKING THE CHOICE

Dr. James MacDonald once said, "Forgiveness is a crisis and a process."[2] You can make a choice to forgive someone who hurt you, but that doesn't mean your emotions have necessarily caught up to your will. When you see that person again—at the mall, on campus, or maybe even at church—it is easy for some of those old bitter feelings to come flooding back again.

The intensity of those feelings may surprise you, and you may think to yourself, *I thought I'd already dealt with that. I thought I'd forgiven him.* Perhaps you did. But forgiveness is an ongoing process as well as an initial moment of crisis. When you see your offender again, you need to shoot up a quick prayer, saying, "Lord, I choose to forgive him. Right now, I'm choosing Your grace over these feelings of anger and bitterness."

Choosing God's grace over your control is the way of escape from the deadly clutches of anger.

That, my friend, is a choice for life and peace.

When you feel yourself becoming angry over a situation, remember that, as we said at the beginning of this chapter, it's because you are feeling a lack of control. That's the time to say, "God, look what has happened to me. I am so angry about it. But I know You have sovereignty over even this, and I choose Your grace, right now, over my control." Then take a deep breath, release your clenched fists, and ask the God who loves you and knows you so well for a fresh infusion of His grace. Choosing God's grace over your control is the way of escape from the deadly clutches of anger.

And when it comes to God's grace, you can be sure of this: He has more than enough for your every need.

SIX

GUILT

When Your Conscience Is Killing You

My guilt overwhelms me—it is a burden too heavy to bear.

*M*acbeth, by William Shakespeare. Have you ever read it? I was assigned to read it in high school. To be sure, I read some of it from Shakespeare, but I read most of it from a guy named Cliff who took notes on it (CliffsNotes). He helped me understand *Macbeth* in a fraction of the time.

Do you remember the play's basic plot? Macbeth had been given a prophecy that he would one day be king of his land, and he thought that sounded pretty good. He liked the idea of being king, but he didn't obsess over it. However, his wife, Lady Macbeth, did. The thought of being queen filled her with fierce desire. In fact, Mrs. Macbeth was so eager for her husband to lay claim to the throne that she plotted the death of the reigning king, Duncan. Macbeth really didn't want to assassinate the king, but his wife goaded him and coaxed him and even provided the daggers so he could dispose of Duncan.

Eventually, they succeeded in their dark deed, and King Duncan was slain. Then they planted the bloody daggers on the king's attendants, framing them for the king's murder. It was a terrible act of cold-blooded treachery.

After the murder and the successful frame job comes the most memorable and perhaps the most famous scene in the play. Lady Macbeth is sleepwalking. Guilt-ridden, she pantomimes washing her hands, and cries, "Out, damned spot! Out, I say. . . . What! Will these hands ne'er be clean? . . . Here's the smell of the blood still: all the perfumes of Arabia will not sweeten this little hand."[1]

At the end of the play, gripped with overwhelming remorse

and an insatiable desire to silence the accuser within her, Lady Macbeth takes her own life.

Guilt is truly a painful, devastating emotion because it bites and gnaws a person's conscience with unrelenting fervor.

Guilt and remorse are Siamese twins, joined at the heart.

Remorse, a synonym for *guilt*, comes from the Latin *remorsus*, combining *re*, which means "again," with *mordere*, meaning "to bite or to gnaw." Put them together and you have a clear picture of guilt. Guilt is truly a painful, devastating emotion because it bites and gnaws a person's conscience with unrelenting fervor. Living with guilt is like being haunted by an evil ghost who constantly reminds you of your past sins.

There's a little poem I like by the Latin poet Juvenal. It says:

> *Trust me, no tortures which the poets feign,*
> *Can match the fierce, the unutterable pain*
> *He feels, who night and day, devoid of rest,*
> *Carries his own accuser within his breast.*[2]

That is guilt in a nutshell. It is torture that produces unutterable pain. Some guilt-ridden souls deal with the unending, unutterable pain by following in the footsteps of Lady Macbeth. They choose the dark and terrible path of suicide. Judas Iscariot, for example, filled with intense remorse for betraying the Lord Jesus Christ, took his own life. As one preacher poignantly said of Judas, "Trying to silence the hell within him, he hanged himself and stepped into the hell before him." Suicide is never the answer, even when your sin is as great as Judas's. But guilt is so powerful that it can drive people to literally destroy themselves.

THE PROBLEM OF UNRESOLVED GUILT

Dr. Hobart Mowrer, psychologist, university professor, and former president of the American Psychological Association, did extensive research into the subject of guilt. He considered it to be a great problem with those in need of counseling. Mowrer said, "While there are substantial indications that some people do have a biochemical disorder that manifests itself in mental abnormalities, the record offers persuasive evidence that much mental illness stems from the old-fashioned toxins of sin and [unresolved] guilt."[3]

Is unresolved guilt a problem for you? Is it eating away at your soul? Is your conscience killing you? Is the ghost of guilt haunting you over something you did—or failed to do—perhaps even years ago? Maybe some sexual sin in your past has never come to light. Or maybe you committed a crime, or had an abortion, or pushed your girlfriend to have an abortion. Maybe you lied about someone, causing that person tremendous difficulty and heartache. Whatever the case, is there something in your heart that points at you and says, "Guilty!"? Something that bites and gnaws at you and won't leave you alone? What's the message when the smoke alarm of guilt starts blaring?

EMOTION: Guilt
WARNING: Your God-given sense of moral uprightness
    is on fire!

The message is simply this: Your God-given sense of moral uprightness is on fire! There is some sin in your life that has violated your God-given conscience and must be faced and dealt with.

GUILT-RIDDEN KING DAVID

By the time King David wrote Psalm 32, he was desperately tired of the unending blare of the smoke alarm within. His sense of moral uprightness was ablaze, and this is why: David had committed adultery with Bathsheba, the wife of one of his most loyal soldiers, Uriah the Hittite. To make matters worse—much worse—Bathsheba ended up pregnant from that one night of unbridled lust. So David, in an attempt to cover his hot-blooded, adulterous sin, compounded his iniquity with cold-blooded, calculated, premeditated murder. He personally orchestrated Uriah's death by putting him in the fiercest part of the battle with the Ammonites and withdrawing the rest of the troops. Uriah didn't stand a chance. David then took Uriah's widow as his wife. The whole sordid story can be read in 2 Samuel 11.

After attempting to cover up this frightful injustice and the great sin he had committed against God, Bathsheba, and her husband, Uriah, David was eventually confronted by the prophet Nathan. In that dramatic encounter, David confessed his great sin to God, and was graciously forgiven. Sometime later, perhaps reflecting back on those darkest of days, David wrote Psalm 32:

How blessed is he whose transgression is forgiven,
whose sin is covered!
How blessed is the man to whom the Lord does not impute iniquity,

and in whose spirit there is no deceit!
When I kept silent about my sin, my body wasted away
through my groaning all day long.
For day and night Your hand was heavy upon me;
my vitality was drained away as with the fever heat of summer. Selah.
I acknowledged my sin to You,
and my iniquity I did not hide;
I said, "I will confess my transgressions to the Lord";
and You forgave the guilt of my sin. Selah. (vv. 1–5)

Two Ways to Deal with Sin and Guilt

David knew better than to do what he did, and his God-given con-science wouldn't leave him alone until he dealt with his sin and settled the matter. The smoke alarm of guilt went on and on and on, until David finally did what was necessary to douse the fire.

It's the same with you and me. If we have something smoldering—or perhaps in open flames—in our conscience, we need to respond to the smoke alarm and take steps to deal with the sin in our lives.

There are two main ways to deal with sin, and both of them are found in Psalm 32. The first way is the world's way, and many people in our culture and our world have followed this decep-tive, destructive path. The second, of course, is God's way.

So, what does the *world* say to do with sin and the corresponding smoke alarm of guilt?

David knew better than to do what he did, and his God-given conscience wouldn't leave him alone until he dealt with his sin and settled the matter.

THE WORLD SAYS, "RATIONALIZE YOUR SIN!"

Refusing to confess and forsake their sin, society tries to rationalize it away. Perhaps David thought he could pull that off, too. Maybe he said to himself, "Hey, you know what? I'm the king, and I have a right to what I want. The rules that other people follow don't really apply to kings, do they? Besides, Bathsheba tempted me. She shouldn't have been bathing on a rooftop, anyway. Any man would have been tempted. And yes, Uriah died in battle. But didn't my general say that 'the sword devours one as well as another'? Who's to say Uriah wouldn't have died that day in battle anyway?" David refused to acknowledge his sin . . . until he couldn't stand it anymore. He had been a man after God's own heart, so it wasn't going to work. He was as wretched and unhappy as a man could be: "When I refused to confess my sin, my body wasted away," he wrote, "and I groaned all day long. Day and night your hand of discipline was heavy on me. My strength evaporated like water in the summer heat" (Ps. 32:3–4 NLT).

Do you know what the word rationalize *sounds like to me? It sounds like* rational lies.

Do you sin and try to rationalize it away? As a pastor, I've heard *many* people in my office try to rationalize their sin:

- "My husband doesn't pay attention to me. He drove me to this affair!"
- "My wife wasn't meeting my needs. It's really her fault."
- "My alcoholism is a disease. It's not my fault!"
- "My parents were angry and yelled at me when I was growing up, so I have a lot of repressed hostility. That's why I have an anger problem."
- "I know I'm living with my boyfriend, but we're in *love*, and that's what counts."

- "Homosexuality isn't a sin if the partners are faithful to each other. Besides, even some church bishops are gay, right?"

Do you know what the word *rationalize* sounds like to me? It sounds like *rational lies*. It's a bunch of lies that sound somewhat reasonable to our own ears, so we hide behind them, just as Adam hid behind that bush in the garden of Eden. When he did finally face God, how did he answer God's question about eating the forbidden fruit? "The *woman* whom You gave to be with me, she gave me from the tree, and I ate" (Gen. 3:12; emphasis added). In effect, Adam was saying, "I'm innocent, God. It's Eve's fault . . . or maybe even *Your* fault, because You gave her to me." Rational lies.

The problem with rationalizing your sin is this: God isn't buying it and neither is your conscience. You can tell your rational lies until the cows come home, but guilt's smoke alarm will continue to blare.

Where does this troublesome sense of morality in our lives come from? It comes from God, our Creator. The apostle John taught us that "God is Light, and in Him there is no darkness at all" (1 John 1:5). What does this God of light say about dark deeds? He calls it *sin*, plain and simple. He doesn't call it a disease or a weakness or a frailty or a sickness or an issue. The true name for any action that transgresses God's law is *sin*. Adultery is sin. Premarital sex is sin. Homosexuality is sin. You can call these things whatever you like, and paint them over with soft pastels, but it doesn't change what they are. You and I don't get to write the rule book; God has already done that. And yes, our society may be changing, but God *never* changes, and His Word is settled forever (see Psalm 119:89).

You and I don't get to write the rule book; God has already done that.

In Proverbs 30:20 we read: "This is the way of an adulterous woman. She eats and wipes her mouth and says, 'I have done no wrong.'" But we all know she has.

Jeremiah 6:15 says, "Were they ashamed because of the abomination they have done? They were not even ashamed at all. They did not even know how to blush." We are in a bad place as individuals—and as a culture—when we live in open sin without any sense of shame, when we don't even know how to blush.

Before we excuse ourselves too quickly, however, we need to look more carefully at our own lives, at some of those "under the radar" sins. We gossip, tell "white" lies, refuse to forgive, lose our tempers, hold on to bitterness in our hearts, speak cutting words to loved ones, watch things we shouldn't on TV, or maybe toy with impure images on our computer.

"Well," we say, "that's different. That's no big deal."

But it is a big deal. These, too, are sins against God, but we cover them over with our rationalizations, our rational lies.

The apostle John wrote: "If we say that we have no sin, we are deceiving ourselves and the truth is not in us. . . . If we say that we have no sin, we make [God] a liar and His Word is not in us" (1 John 1:8, 10).

What's the bottom line here? You can go the way of the world if you want to, and rationalize and justify your sins against God. But if you do, don't expect to walk with Him or have fellowship with Him. You'll be on your own, which is a frightening place to be.

THE WORLD SAYS, "HIDE YOUR SIN!"

Another way the world deals with sin is to simply cover it over and hide it away. David wrote, "I kept silent about my sin . . ." (Ps. 32:3). The word *silent* in the Hebrew means "to be dumb, to be speechless, to be deaf." It was as if David threw a sheet over his transgressions, and pretended they weren't there. He took all of his lust, adultery, deception, and murder, pushed them into a dark closet, closed the door, and denied they were even there. He kept silent about his wrongdoing.

You will most likely have physical pain and problems if you try to paper over your sin and pretend that it's not there.

But the remorse kept biting and gnawing away at him, day after day, week after week. He would walk around the palace sighing and groaning, and when someone said, "What's the matter, King David?" he would say, "Nothing. Nothing at all." All the while, however, his unconfessed sin was eating him alive. In Psalm 38:3, he wrote: "There is no health in my bones because of my sin."

The Pain of Cover-Up

The lesson here is that you will most likely have physical pain and problems if you try to paper over your sin and pretend it's not there. That's what Lady Macbeth tried to do, but she couldn't get it out of her mind and off her conscience. Even at night she would sleepwalk, trying to wash the blood from her hands.

Some people suffer insomnia, colitis, ulcers, or eating disorders because they're trying to hide their sin. Others have nervous breakdowns and suicidal thoughts.

Many years ago, I watched an interesting interview on *The Oprah Winfrey Show*. Oprah was talking to a woman who had been trapped in the sex industry, making hard-core pornographic movies. Oprah asked her to tell her story and how she got out.

The woman's account was so vivid that I will never forget it. She said something to this effect: "One day, I was taking a shower, trying desperately to get clean. But no matter how hard I tried, I couldn't wash off the filth." Before finally escaping from this terrible lifestyle, she suffered two nervous breakdowns, and tried to kill herself on two separate occasions.

When I heard that interview, I thought about this scripture: "No amount of soap or lye can make you clean. You are stained with guilt that cannot ever be washed away. I see it always before me, the Lord God says" (Jer. 2:22 TLB).

THE PRESSURE OF COVER-UP

There's pain associated with hiding your sin and trying to call it something else. But there is also *pressure*. David wrote, "Day and night Your hand was heavy upon me; my vitality was drained away as with the fever heat of summer" (Ps. 32:4). He was under tremendous inner pressure that seemed to be squeezing the very life out of him. At night, when he tried to sleep, it felt as though he had an elephant sitting on his chest.

In His great love for David, God couldn't let this go on and on. He couldn't allow David to go on pretending to be in relationship with Him, acting as if everything was fine. If David was going to continually refuse to fall down before the Lord and confess, God would have to break him. We know that because in Psalm 51, written after David had been forgiven and restored, the king wrote, "Let me hear joy and gladness; let the bones you have crushed rejoice" (v. 8 NIV).

David was a child of God who really knew and loved the Lord.

The Bible describes him as a man after God's own heart (see Acts 13:22). David knew what it was to worship the Lord, sing to Him, dance before Him, and sit in awe before Him. He had a genuine relationship with Yahweh God. The trouble was that after he'd fallen out of fellowship and was no longer walking in the light, he continued to *act* like God's friend in a fake, hypocritical way.

And God says, "*That doesn't work for Me.*"

So God's hand was heavy on David, and He began to crush him until he dealt with that phony pretense.

When I first got saved, one of the ways I knew my salvation was genuine was what happened to me after I sinned. Oh man, was God's hand heavy on me! I'd never experienced anything like it before. Whenever I did some of the things I used to do before I met Christ, conviction would come into my heart. It was the finger of God, penetrating my heart and saying, "*Jeff, that was a lie. Jeff, that was lust. Jeff, you're holding on to bitterness. You need to deal with these things. I'm not going to let it go.*" Like David, I experienced and still experience pressure from the Lord over unconfessed, unaddressed sin.

The writer of Hebrews didn't mince words regarding this subject: "It is for discipline that you endure; God deals with you as with sons; for what son is there whom his father does not discipline? But if you are without discipline, of which all have become partakers, then you are illegitimate children and not sons" (12:7–8).

It's as plain as day. God says, "*If you're not experiencing discipline, then you're not My child.*" If you can sleep around, have sex with your girlfriend or boyfriend, get drunk on the weekends, or harbor bitterness and

It's as plain as day. God says, "If you're not experiencing discipline, then you're not My child."

hatred toward another person, and say, "Really, it doesn't bother me," do you know *why* it doesn't bother you? Because God is not your Father. You are lost. *That* is why it doesn't bother you. *That* is why you don't feel any pressure.

God deals with Christians as His own sons and daughters, and that relationship comes with the Father's discipline, to keep us on the right path. Sin brings pain for everybody, but sin brings *pressure* on the child of God when he or she tries to hide it, ignore it, or wallpaper over it.

In this sense, the smoke alarm of guilt is a blessing. It *ought to* be sounding if you're out of fellowship with your heavenly Father. The alarm *ought to* be making a racket if you have offended the Spirit of God. It's when that alarm goes silent that you need to be concerned.

Trying to hide your sin from the Lord is so very foolish. After David's adultery and murder, 2 Samuel 11:27 tells us that "the thing that David had done was evil in the sight of the LORD." God saw everything the king did, from the moment he lingered too long on his rooftop, peering down at a woman taking a bath, to Uriah's death at David's command. God sees and God knows. His eyes miss nothing, as the Bible declares again and again.

> For a man's ways are in full view of the Lord,
> and he examines all his paths. (Prov. 5:21 NIV)

> The eyes of the Lord are in every place,
> Watching the evil and the good. (Prov. 15:3)

> And there is no creature hidden from His sight, but all things are
> open and laid bare to the eyes of Him with whom we have to do.
> (Heb. 4:13)

If you go the world's path in regard to sin, it will bring death. You will constantly be haunted by the ghost of guilt, and you won't be able to escape from those gnawing, biting feelings of remorse.

But you and I don't have to go that way—not at all. There's a second way to go, and that's God's way.

GOD SAYS, "REPENT OF YOUR SIN, AND I WILL FORGIVE YOU."

David began Psalm 32 with the words: "How blessed is he whose transgression is forgiven, whose sin is covered. How blessed is the man to whom the LORD does not impute iniquity and in whose spirit there is no deceit."

How *blessed*. In other words, "How happy."

How do you experience that blessed happiness?

God's way of dealing with sin involves three elements:

- acknowledging your sin,
- confessing your sin, and
- believing God's Word—not your feelings—regarding your sin.

1. ACKNOWLEDGE YOUR SIN

In Psalm 32:5, David wrote: "I acknowledged my sin to You, and my iniquity I did not hide." That's the very first step. The word *acknowledge* is translated from the Hebrew word that means "to know," "to know fully," or "to know intimately." What does that mean? It means you pull your sin out of the darkness and let God's light shine on it. You take it out of the corner of the closet, and remove the sheet that's covering it over. Then you say, "This is what I did. In all its ugliness, this is it."

People don't like to do that. They don't like to soberly look in the mirror with the lights on full and see what is truly there. They would rather just walk in the darkness. You and I are the same way. We like to cover over sins, just as we might try to cover over a blemish on our faces. I've been on TV a couple of times, and before you go on camera, makeup artists put you in a room, and man, they can do wonders! I asked one of them, "Hey, can you make it look as if I have hair?" She said, "No, we can do a lot, but we can't do that." Even so, the makeup covers over wrinkles and blemishes and all sorts of other unsightly things. And that's what we would rather do with our sins! Cover them up, and pretend like they're not really there.

If you're going to acknowledge your sin to God, you take off the masks, remove the makeup, and say, "God, this is what it was; and it's horrible and shameful."

Sometimes we'll do that with our words. Instead of admitting to road rage, we'll say, "Well, I have an issue with anger sometimes." Or, instead of coming clean about adultery, we'll say, "I made a mistake," or, "I had a lapse in moral judgment," or, "I made some unwise choices." No, what you did was have sex with someone *other than* your own spouse. What you did was adultery, betrayal of your vows, and a great offense before the God who loves you.

If you're going to acknowledge your sin to God, you take off the masks, remove the makeup, and say, "This is what it was; and it's horrible, it's gross, it's shameful, and it's ugly." You name it before the Lord in an open recognition of sin.

2. Honestly Confess Your Sin

After you've pulled the sheet off your sin, you're ready for the second step: confessing your sin. That's when you say, "God, I agree with You that this is sin. It was wrong, and I am so sorry I did that. Not only did I break Your law, God, but I also broke Your heart."

David said, "I will confess my transgressions to the LORD." The Hebrew word David used for *confess* means "to cast down, to throw down." It's a picture of getting that thing out of your life and turning away from it. In other words, it's a picture of repentance. We are saying to the Lord, "I don't want that in my life, Lord. I am throwing it down."

In the New Testament, the Greek term used for *confession* means "to say the same thing as." In other words, it means to *agree* with God. When you confess your sin, you are saying the same thing about it that God says—that it is awful, harmful, treasonous, and even deadly.

What happens then? According to those incredibly liberating words in 1 John 1:9: "If we confess our sins, He is faithful and righteous to forgive us our sins and to cleanse us from all unrighteousness."

But note this: there's a big *if* in that verse.

If we confess our sins, He will forgive us. But *if* we don't, He won't. And *if* we are walking in unconfessed, unrepented, and unforgiven sin, then we are walking in darkness and living a lie. We may say we have fellowship with God, but we really don't.

You may say, "But I *have* confessed my sins, and I *have* received God's forgiveness. Why do I still feel so guilty sometimes?" That brings us to a third step.

3. BELIEVE GOD'S WORD—OVER YOUR FEELINGS

"I said, 'I will confess my transgressions to the LORD'; and You forgave the guilt of my sin."

PSALM 32:3 (EMPHASIS ADDED)

What was true for David is true for you and me. Again, 1 John 1:9 says that if we confess our sins, God will "cleanse us from all unrighteousness."

Did you see that little word "all"? *All* means *all.* All is forgiven, no matter what you've done. He *will* cleanse you from *all* of it. That homosexual act . . . that abortion . . . that betrayal . . . that divorce . . . that dishonesty. Whatever it is, He will cleanse you. And that is the point where you must believe God's Word more than you believe your own feelings.

If you are going to walk in victory over guilt and being haunted by the sins of your past, you must believe God's Word!

Why? Because the devil, named in Scripture as "the accuser of our brethren" and "the father of lies" (Rev. 12:10; John 8:44), will whisper to your heart, "There's no way you're forgiven. Have you forgotten what you've done? Do you really think you're washed clean inside? Really? Can I replay the tape of what you did? Can I show you all the damage and hurt that you've caused? And you have the audacity to say you're forgiven? You have the nerve to stand up in church and sing, 'My chains are gone, I've been set free . . .'?"

What you need to know in that instant, what you must understand, is that the voice you're hearing is not conviction from God; it's an accusation, a poison arrow, from an enemy who hates you and wants to destroy you. But if you are going to walk in victory

154

over guilt and being haunted by the sins of your past, *you must believe God's Word!*

What makes this especially challenging is that the enemy's lies fit hand in hand with our feelings, prompting our flesh to rise up and say, "That's right. I have confessed my sins, but since I still don't *feel* forgiven, God's promise to forgive me must not be enough. I've got to do something else, in addition to my confession, to really get forgiveness." That's the scenario men like Martin Luther got into, hundreds of years ago, when men under the conviction of sin would beat themselves bloody, walk on their knees for miles, and even crawl over broken glass, thinking that somehow they were repaying God for their sins by shedding their own blood.

Don't fall into the devil's trap of elevating your sin over God's Son.

But we don't have to shed blood for our own sins. There is One who already bled for us. His name is Jesus. John wrote, "If we walk in the light, as He Himself is in the light . . . the blood of Jesus, God's Son, *cleanses us from all sin*" (1 John 1:6–7; emphasis added).

Don't fall into the devil's trap of elevating your sin over God's Son. The blood of Jesus cleanses us completely and totally from all sin *if* we acknowledge, confess, get things right, and come His way. And the Bible tells us, "What God has cleansed, no longer consider unholy" (Acts 10:15).

CONFESSIONS: PRIVATE AND PUBLIC

Sometimes people come before God, agree with Him about their sin, receive His forgiveness—and then turn right around and do the same thing again! Inside, they'll groan, and say, *Oh no! I can't believe this. I did it again. How can I go back to the Lord again (so soon) and ask for forgiveness? What am I going to do?*

When this happens to us, especially if it happens more than once, we begin to feel like a hamster in a wheel, going around and around but never getting anywhere.

Is this something we have to just live with? Repeating the same pattern and falling into the same trap over and over? No, God wants you out of that hamster wheel. He wants you to turn from your sins, and not go back to them.

But Scripture also says that God understands our weakness: "He is mindful that we are but dust" (Ps. 103:14). Knowing these things, He has given us a strong weapon to help us escape from habitual, repetitive sins. The answer is found in James 5:16, where we read, "Confess your sins to one another, and pray for one another, that you may be healed."

Now, do we like to do this? Of course not. Who wants to tell someone else about a habitual weakness or an area of sin that has a grip on his life? It's embarrassing. And we would rather people think we don't have any problems or struggles. One man doesn't want to tell another man that he keeps getting caught in the web of pornography. One woman doesn't want to tell another woman about her sexual fantasies, or her jealousy, or some other troubling sin. We don't want to do it. We tell ourselves we don't really *need* to do it, and that we can win the battle "on our own." But then we fall again . . . and again . . . and feel so discouraged and defeated.

But James says, in so many words, "Do you want to be healed? Then bring a trusted brother or sister into your confidence. Admit your sins to one another, pray for each other, and hold each other accountable week by week."

PUBLIC SINS, PUBLIC CONFESSION

Dr. Hobart Mowrer said this: "Until one has worked through and resolved his guilt in the face of all mankind, he is not fully healed and whole."[4]

Private sins only require private confession, to the Lord and a trusted friend. Public sins that are widespread, however, must be dealt with differently. If you have sinned publicly, you need to confess publicly. When the truth came out about pro golfer Tiger Woods's multiple adulteries, he faced the cameras on national TV and apologized to the world. Woods is a Buddhist, not a Christian, but he stood in the glare of those TV lights and flashbulbs, owned up to what he had done, and said he was sorry.

> *"Until one has worked through and resolved his guilt in the face of all mankind, he is not fully healed and whole."*
>
> *—Hobart Mowrer*

Yes, what he did was tragic, shameful, degrading, and revealed deep character issues in his life. But my opinion of him went up when he looked the nation in the eyes and said he was wrong and that his behavior was inexcusable. Let's face it. There are many Christians in the public eye who need to follow Tiger's example, yet they rarely do.

RILEY AND TRACEY

I love the true story about a couple I'll call Riley and Tracey, one of the finest young couples in their church. These two young people loved the Lord and walked with God, and the church knew it. They were engaged to be married and were planning a big church wedding. It was going to be a huge event, and the whole church was invited. Riley and Tracey wanted to let everyone know they intended to build their home on the Rock, Jesus Christ.

A couple of weeks before the wedding, however, Riley and Tracey asked to meet with the senior pastor. They sat down in his office and said to him, "Pastor, we have something to confess. Tracey's pregnant." They were brokenhearted and repentant, and in no way tried to justify what they had done.

Riley said, "What we did was a sin. And now we're going to get married in a few weeks in front of everybody, but Tracey's pregnant."

The pastor said quietly, "What do you think God wants you to do?"

"We've talked about this," Riley replied, "and I believe God wants me to stand before the church and confess my sin. I want them to learn this situation from me, and not from some rumor. If they all come to the wedding and then learn what we've done, our testimony for Christ will be worthless. We wanted our wedding to be a witness to our families. We wanted to let everyone know what we stood for and stand for, but now all that is ruined. But if we don't confess it ourselves, it will only be worse. We will be hypocrites."

So the pastor said, "I think that's wise."

The next Sunday night, Riley got up with his wife-to-be there by his side, and courageously, repentantly confessed their sin before the congregation.

And what did the church do? Disown them? Hate them? Pick up stones to stone them?

No. They forgave them.

After the meeting, one of the ladies said, "Riley, I've known you all your life, and I've been so proud of you as I've watched you grow up, and as I've watched you walk with God. But I have never been more proud of you than I am right now."

So the church embraced them, and said, "God has forgiven you, and we forgive you." There was victory that night in the lives of Riley and Tracey, and in that church.

A couple of weeks later, when the bride and groom stood together at the altar, their hearts were pure, knowing they weren't trying to hide their secret sin, hoping against hope no one would find out or guess.

THE POWER OF CONFESSION

If you want to see the chains of private sins broken, find someone you can trust, be open about your sin with him or her, and meet often enough to hold each other accountable. Scripture says that if you do this, *you will be healed.* And if you have sinned publicly, where people know that you've done something terrible, don't play-act like nothing's happened. Follow the example of that young man Riley. Stand up. Face the music. Most people will forgive you, love you, and embrace you. Most of God's people really *want* to do that; they *want* to forgive.

It's pure speculation of course, but I wonder what would have happened if Richard Nixon had gone before the nation as soon as the rumors of the Watergate scandal began to rumble. What if there had been no attempt at all of a cover-up? What if he had confessed to the nation, and said, "I've let you down, and I've disgraced this office. Please forgive me." Would he still have felt compelled to resign from office? Possibly, but our national wounds would have healed much more quickly, and many people would have admired a president who was big enough to look America in the eye and admit his mistakes.

You and I don't have to live with the biting and gnawing of remorse. When we fail, falter, stumble, and fall into sin (and by the way, all of us do), we can reject the world's hypocritical method of dealing with iniquity. We can go to the Lord and have our hearts made new again.

The psalmist wrote in Psalm 130:3–4:

> If You, LORD, should mark iniquities,
> O Lord, who could stand?
> But there is forgiveness with You,
> That You may be feared.

And to that I can add only one word . . . Amen.

SEVEN

DISCONTENTMENT

Unhappy Campers

*I have learned to be content in whatever
circumstances I am.*

PHILIPPIANS 4:11

It was spring break 1998. I was all fired up to take my family on a big spring break vacation to Colorado to play in the snow (the girls were ten, eight, and six at the time). Living in Texas as we do, we'd never been around very much snow, and none of us knew how to ski. Even so, we wanted to experience the white stuff as a family, do some sledding, and have a little fun.

For a pastor's family, this was an expensive trip. When you started adding up airfare, car rental, meals, and renting a condo for a whole week . . . this vacation was the biggest one we had ever taken. Since spending money does not come easily for me, I wanted this to be a *great* experience for the whole family.

After picking up the car in Denver, we drove to snowy Breckenridge and found our condo. It was on the third floor. By the time we'd wrestled our luggage up three flights of stairs in that thin air, Debbie and I fell on the couch, exhausted and needing an oxygen tank.

The kids had gone downstairs to play in the snow, and when we finally joined them, we didn't encounter the happy, Norman Rockwell scene we had anticipated. Amy, our eight-year-old, was crying her eyes out. She had snow in her boots and had lost one of her gloves. She was freezing to death.

"I w-want to go h-home," she sobbed.

Go home? We'd only been in the Colorado snow for less than an hour, and she was ready to bail on this expensive vacation of a lifetime. (Have I told you how I don't like to spend money?) Trying to keep the mood positive, I said, "Hey, we're going to go sledding now, and it'll be lots of fun. You'll see."

But where do you go to sled? We didn't know. So we got in the car and started driving around, looking for a hill. Within minutes, I was lost. Then, trying to turn the car around in a cul-de-sac, I got the car stuck in the snow.

That's when Debbie started laughing. She does that when she's a little tense. Let's just say the timing of her giggles isn't always the best for me.

As I sat in the car, stuck in the snow with Debbie nervously giggling, I felt like crying along with Amy, "I wanna go home, too!" I kept thinking to myself, *How much money have I spent for this miserable vacation?* I could have stayed home and cleaned out the garage for a whole lot less. The dream vacation was quickly turning into a nightmare.

> *Someone has well described the emotion of discontentment as a combination of sadness, frustration, irritation, and disappointment with your current situation in life.*

Stuck in a cul-de-sac. Looking back now, I realize that was a perfect picture of where my life was at that time. Because I had allowed a series of negative circumstances to sour my heart, I was now stuck in a morass of discontentment. I needed my car out of the snow—and my heart out of the snow—so the joy could flow again.

Can you relate to the feeling of discontentment?

"I CAN'T GET NO . . ."

Someone has well described the emotion of discontentment as a combination of sadness, frustration, irritation, and disappointment with your current situation in life. Did you catch that? The ugly feelings of discontentment are directly related to your attitude regarding your present circumstances. Without question, a discontented person is experiencing circumstances he deems undesirable, unacceptable, and unwanted. And no matter how much good may be present with the bad, all he sees is the bad. That is exactly what I did on my Colorado vacation. Rather than focus on the joys of my family and the beauty of Colorado, I focused on the miseries of being stuck in the snow. My attitude regarding my current circumstances was poor, to say the least.

To be sure, we all struggle with feelings of discontentment from time to time. But for some, discontentment is their forwarding address and way of life. No matter what is going on around them, it's just never good enough. You know how it goes . . . if you're single, you keep wishing you were married. And then you get married and find yourself looking back with nostalgia on your "carefree" single days. (I have heard marriage compared to flies on a windowpane. Those outside are trying to get in . . . and those inside are trying to get out.)

Some people become discontented with their jobs, or their homes, or their church, or even with their favorite football team when it isn't doing so well. Whatever the case, when you're discontented, your focus is on your undesirable circumstances. Rather than looking for silver linings, all you see are the black clouds. As a result, you become edgy, irritable, and negative. You end up with a sour, unhappy countenance.

In short, you become an unhappy camper. Not the sort of person many want to be around, much less join for a vacation.

Are you discontented today with something in your life?

Back in 1965, the Rolling Stones released a pop song called "(I Can't Get No) Satisfaction" that became a monster, number one hit all over the world. *"I can't get no satisfaction . . .'Cause I try and I try and I try and I try."* It was a catchy tune, all right, but I wonder if the popularity of the song had more to do with its theme than its distinctive, fuzz-box guitar riff.

"No satisfaction" is the way many people live. In fact, some people imagine that to be the normal state of affairs—always discontented, unhappy, and dissatisfied. They are constantly disappointed with the way things turn out, and ever reaching for an elusive "something more" that they can never seem to find.

How are we to view these ugly feelings of discontentment that tend to sweep across our souls, trying to make a permanent nest in our hearts? We ought to view them as a smoke alarm telling us that our God-given desire for personal peace and happiness is on fire.

EMOTION: Discontentment

WARNING: Your God-given desire for personal
peace and happiness is on fire.

The Bible speaks of the Lord as the "blessed and only Sovereign" (1 Tim. 6:15). The word *blessed* in Scripture, *makarios* in the Greek, literally means *happy*. God is a happy God, a cheerful Sovereign, who is at complete peace with Himself. When He created us in His own image, He placed within us a desire for happiness, peace, and contentment. Regardless of how hard some people may try, they just can't get rid of the notion that life *ought* to be peaceful and happy. There is a God-given desire within us for tranquility. When we are discontented, we know—in the core of our being—that something isn't right. But what is that *something*, and what can be done to remedy the problem?

When the smoke alarm of discontentment starts to blare, God is trying to tell us that our focus has gone afoul. We are looking to external circumstances to make us happy when we need to be looking to Him. Furthermore, we have lost our sense of gratitude. We have lost sight of the blessings we do have, and have chosen to fixate on that which we don't have. As one preacher so eloquently stated, "Contentment is not getting what you want, but wanting what you already have."

One of the best examples of a contented man is the apostle Paul. From his life, you and I can learn how to silence the smoke alarm of discontentment and extinguish those damaging flames.

Paul's Take on Contentment

Some writers need special surroundings to give them inspiration— a cabin up in the mountains or a bungalow by the beach, or maybe just soft lighting and a comfortable chair with pleasant background music. I can think of at least one literary masterpiece that didn't have the benefit of any of those inspiring conditions.

Although Mick Jagger and the Rolling Stones couldn't "get no satisfaction," Paul had satisfaction that no one could take away!

When the apostle Paul penned his famous letter to the Philippians, he wasn't at the beach or in the mountains. There was no soothing sound of crashing waves or babbling brooks in the background, no peaceful breeze wafting through the trees.

To the contrary, Paul was under house arrest in Rome, chained 24/7 to a Roman guard. Furthermore, he stayed there two full years, in chains and under guard. To top it off, Paul wasn't sure if he would live or die when the time came to appear before Caesar. Can the conditions get much worse?

In the final chapter of his letter to the Philippians, he wrote, "But I rejoice in the Lord greatly, that now at last you have revived your concern for me. Indeed, you were concerned before, but you lacked opportunity" (4:10). The Philippians had sent a gift to help him financially, and that tangible expression of their concern and care for him really lifted his heart. But then he added this comment: "Not that I speak from want, for I have learned to be content in whatever circumstances I am. I know how to get along with humble means, and I also know how to live in prosperity. In any and every circumstance I have learned the secret of being filled and going hungry, both of having abundance and suffering need. I can do all things through Him who strengthens me" (vv. 11–13).

Although Mick Jagger and the Rolling Stones couldn't "get no satisfaction," Paul had satisfaction that no one could take away! He discovered the very secret of satisfaction and learned how to silence the smoke alarm of discontentment. Notice that he said he had *learned* to be content. That is so important to note because if he learned it, you and I can learn it too. I want to share with you three lessons that will help you regain your contentment, no matter what's going on in your life, enabling you to experience joy and peace in great abundance.

LESSON #1: TO ENJOY CONTENTMENT REGARDLESS OF THE CIRCUMSTANCES, RECOGNIZE *WHY* YOU EXPERIENCE DIFFICULT THINGS.

I don't know too many people who express discontentment while walking on the sunny side of the street, experiencing success and prosperity. Discontentment usually comes with difficulties and hardships, not blessings and plenty. When you're finding fulfillment in your job and happiness in your marriage, when your kids are successful and happy, and your grandkids are even better than that, when you're healthy and strong and financially sound . . . you're feeling pretty good about life, right? You are a happy person when everything in your life is coming up roses. And why wouldn't you be?

When the wind changes, however, and you feel the chill of discontentment, it's normally because some of those good things have begun to unravel, right before your eyes. The fact is, *nobody* lives a trouble-free life on this side of heaven. As Job lamented, "Man who is born of a woman is few of days and full of trouble" (Job 14:1 ESV). Jesus echoed this same truth to His disciples: "In the world you have tribulation, but take courage; I have overcome the world" (John 16:33).

You and I are going to have trouble and tribulation in this life here on earth. There is no getting around that fact. Paul said, "Through many tribulations we must enter the kingdom of God" (Acts 14:22). So difficulties will come. We can count on that.

But *why* do the difficulties come? Why does a good God, who loves us, allow such negative things to enter our experience? When troubles suddenly crash into our lives—perhaps blindsiding us—we often find ourselves asking these very questions. "What's up with this?" we say to the Lord. "Don't You care what's happening to me? Don't You love me? Don't You see what's going on? Why would You allow this to come into my life? Are you mad at me, God? What did I do to deserve this?" And we say to ourselves in bewilderment, "This is so strange. Stuff like this shouldn't be happening to me!"

> *The Bible says that trials come into our lives to test us and make us stronger.*

Scripture, however, says that these things aren't really strange at all. As a matter of fact, the Bible says that trials come into our lives to *test* us and make us stronger. In 1 Peter 4:12, we read, "Beloved, do not be surprised at the fiery ordeal among you, which comes upon you for your *testing*, as though some strange thing were happening to you" (emphasis added).

Trials aren't strange. Testing isn't either. These things may be distressful, hurtful, and unwanted . . . but there's nothing strange or out of the ordinary about them. And they actually make us stronger! James wrote, "Consider it all joy, my brethren, when you encounter various trials, knowing that the testing of your faith produces endurance" (James 1:2–3).

The simple truth is this: A faith that can't be tested can't be trusted.

Many times, however, we don't "consider it all joy." In fact, we have trouble considering it *any* joy at all. Why is that? It's because we so easily lose sight of why our sovereign God has allowed these difficulties to enter our lives. Are they just to hurt us or make our lives a misery? Certainly not. They're for our testing and training, to add muscle to our faith and make us stronger in spirit.

The simple truth is this: A faith that can't be tested can't be trusted. If you say, "I have faith in the Lord Jesus Christ," but that faith is never tested, how do you know you have a faith at all? And how can God make us strong spiritually if we never have to exercise our faith or put it into practice? How does He make us men and women who trust Him, regardless of the circumstances? How will He equip us for the challenges and difficult times of tomorrow if He doesn't allow us to walk through hardships today?

THE WEIGHT ROOM

Can you imagine someone just wishing himself into a sleek, strong, muscular body? Go ahead and wish away, but it won't happen! You get big biceps and triceps and six-pack abs by pushing your muscles and building them up. You have to spend time in the weight room. You can't just drive by the gym (on your way to the ice-cream parlor) and say, "I've had my workout now, because I've driven by the gym where they keep all those weights and cardio machines." No, you have to pay the price for a membership, go to the gym, and start lifting.

If you want results, that is.

If you don't want results, then just buy the membership and put the card up on your mantel. Tell yourself how good and disciplined you are for spending fifty bucks a month on a membership you never use.

There's an NFL player for the Washington Redskins named Brian Orakpo. The media call him "the Beast." As a freshman defensive player for the Texas Longhorns, Brian weighed in at 210 pounds. Then the coaches got him in the weight room—and kept him there week after week, month after month, year after year. When Brian Orakpo graduated from the University of Texas, he weighed 260 pounds—with only 8 percent body fat. He gained fifty pounds of pure muscle during those years at Texas.

How did the coaches put fifty pounds on Brian? Did they take him to the endless buffet at Golden Corral, and say, "Eat up, Brian. We need to put some weight on your frame . . . and make sure to load up on the desserts"? Certainly not. That would have been the easy, undisciplined way to gain weight, and it would have been all fat, not muscle. That would have been the way to earn the nickname "the Blob," not "the Beast." What Orakpo did wasn't easy at all. It was extremely difficult, challenging, painful . . . but so rewarding.

Today, Brian Orakpo, at six foot three, 263 pounds, bench presses 515 pounds, squats more than 600 pounds, and does 380 pounds on the clean and jerk. He has a forty-inch vertical jump, and he runs a 4.6-second 40-yard dash.

God trains you and me through our trials and difficulties. That is where we build spiritual muscle.

Pretty amazing! And how did it happen? Well, it didn't happen overnight. He didn't just go into the weight room once or twice a quarter. He spent countless hours there every week, pushing his body to the limit so he could experience the wonderful results.

How does God develop spiritual Brian Orakpos? He does it by taking His sons and daughters through trials, because the testing of your faith produces endurance. It's the testing of your spiritual muscles that makes them strong.

That's something to keep in mind during the hard times, when discontentment sweeps over you, and you wonder, *Why am I going through all this stuff? Why am I stuck in the snow in Colorado? Why is my eight-year-old crying and saying she wants to go home when I've spent all this money on her?* Remember: It's a trial. God is testing you.

But it's not only a test; it's also a teaching opportunity. God allows trials to come into our lives to teach us. The apostle Paul had tremendous, even crushing, trials in his life, and they were all given to teach him. Listen to part of God's "lesson plan" in Paul's life:

> I have worked harder than any of [my fellow ministers]. I have served more prison sentences! I have been beaten times without number. I have faced death again and again.

I have been beaten the regulation thirty-nine stripes by the Jews five times.

I have been beaten with rods three times. I have been stoned once. I have been shipwrecked three times. I have been twenty-four hours in the open sea.

In my travels I have been in constant danger from rivers and floods, from bandits, from my own countrymen, and from pagans. I have faced danger in city streets, danger in the desert, danger on the high seas, danger among false Christians. I have known exhaustion, pain, long vigils, hunger and thirst, going without meals, cold and lack of clothing. (2 Cor. 11:23–27 PHILLIPS)

As if that weren't difficult enough, in the very next chapter, he spoke about a test that really pushed him to the edge. Here's how he described it: "There was given me a thorn in the flesh, a messenger of Satan to torment me—to keep me from exalting myself! Concerning this I implored the Lord three times that it might leave from me" (2 Cor. 12:7–8).

So, did God take it away? No; He said to Paul, "My grace is sufficient for you, for power is perfected in weakness" (v. 9a).

You and I may not always appreciate that sort of answer from God in a time of distress and pain, but to Paul it was a tremendous revelation. In response he said, "Most gladly, therefore, I will rather boast about my weaknesses, that the power of Christ may dwell in me" (v. 9b).

God allowed all those things to come to Paul to teach him that His grace is always sufficient. No matter what might be happening in life, His grace is enough, more than enough.

We don't know what Paul's thorn in the flesh was, but when the Bible speaks about this affliction, it's not talking about a little thorn you would find on a rosebush. The Greek word for "thorn" used here is more like a stake on which you could be impaled. It isn't a little splinter in your thumb; it's a spear in your side, and Paul felt it go right through him. It *hurt*, and he didn't want it in his life anymore. Some people have speculated that he had some distressing condition of the eyes, or perhaps some kind of disfiguring disease. We don't know exactly what it was, but we do know that it was terribly difficult for the apostle. Yet through that agonizing struggle God taught him, *"My grace is enough for you, Paul. It's all you need."*

And it is all we need as well, regardless of what trials may come our way.

Lesson #2: To Enjoy Contentment Regardless of the Circumstances, You Need to Realize What You Can Experience in Jesus Christ.

When Paul wrote, "I've learned to be *content*," the word he used literally meant "self-sufficient." In other words, Paul was saying, "Apart from anything external, without any outside help, I have within me the secret of contentment." And what was that secret? It was Jesus Christ living within him.

The life of Jesus within us, then, is the secret of overcoming any external circumstances in which we may find ourselves. Maybe you're reading these words and saying, "But Jeff, you don't understand. We're about to go under. Our finances are in ruins! Now, if somebody would just drop some money on us—say, fifty thousand dollars—that would clear up everything, and we'd be out of hot water and flying high. That's all we need—a little outside help to get us out of this jam and lift us out of this deep hole of discontentment."

Paul took the opposite approach. His message was, "Friends,

I have joy and contentment in my life right now, and believe me, it's *not* based on externals and outward circumstances! It's based on Jesus. *He* is the secret to overcoming any and every situation." Scripture says, "I am ready for anything through the strength of the one who lives within me" (Phil. 4:13 PHILLIPS).

Paul is telling us, "When I have a little, just enough to get by, it's okay. I'm sufficient in Jesus. When I have an abundance, that's okay too. I'll take it. But the truth is, either way my contentment won't change, because it isn't based on those external things. My joy isn't based on the

Money talks. It says, "Good-bye."

fact that I have a lot of money in the bank or that my 401(k) is holding steady or that my portfolio is doing great in the stock market. My joy is based on having the Lord of joy enthroned in my heart."

What is *your* joy based on?

Many people today base their joy on finances. (No wonder so many people look depressed!) If I'm doing well financially, I'm happy, and I've got a smile on my face. When you think about it, however, that's a pretty flimsy platform on which to build your hope and peace. Someone has said, "Money talks," and I agree with that. Money does talk. It says, "Good-bye!" Wise King Solomon wrote: "Do not weary yourself to gain wealth. Cease from your consideration of it. When you set your eyes on it, it is gone. For wealth certainly makes itself wings, like an eagle that flies toward the heavens" (Prov. 23:4–5).

Others will say, "I'm building my joy around my marriage and my family. That's where I'll find my happiness and contentment." Well, what happens when a loved one dies? Or when there is an unwanted divorce? Will you still be content when family members move far away, and you only get to see them once or twice each year?

Maybe you're counting on good health and physical strength to bring contentment. You jog three miles a day, drink vegetable juice, and eat tofu. That's all well and good because it feels wonderful to feel wonderful . . . but it is also very unpredictable. Physical health can be here today and gone tomorrow.

Just recently, I read about the actor known as "Mr. T." Remember him? His real name is Laurence Tureaud. He is a former bouncer, former bodyguard, and all-around tough guy. Back in the '80s and '90s, he was a popular celebrity who sported a signature Mohawk and multiple gold chains around his neck. He gained fame in the 1982 movie *Rocky III*, playing the seemingly invincible opponent, James "Clubber" Lang. On TV, he was in the hit show *The A-Team*, as Sergeant Bosco "B. A." Baracus ("B. A." stood for Bad Attitude, and Mr. T. certainly fit the bill). He was as menacing, powerful, and intimidating as they come.

Then, in the midst of all his success and physical invincibility, he got cancer. The disease and the chemo cure made him as weak as a kitten and as sick as a dog. Mr. T was quoted as saying, "You know, it didn't matter how much money I had. It didn't matter how strong I was physically. It didn't matter how many gold chains I had. None of that meant anything when I got cancer."

Your contentment can overflow every single day, no matter what the outward circumstances of your life might be.

What is the lesson to be learned from Mr. T? You can't build your joy and contentment on health, because it could all change with your very next heartbeat.

What else is there? Sports teams? All I can say is, it's a good thing my sense of well-being doesn't depend on how well the Texas Long-horns perform in a given football season, or I might be one very unhappy camper.

The apostle Paul, though, learned the secret of contentment—even in prison, with a possible death sentence hanging over his head, and even with a distressing thorn in the flesh that never went away. The secret is finding your joy in Jesus Christ.

Finances change; families change; neighborhoods change; health conditions change; good looks change; opportunities change; earthly relationships change; careers change; even churches change . . . but Jesus never changes. He is "the same yesterday and today and forever" (Heb. 13:8). That means—just think of it!—that your contentment can overflow every single day, no matter what the outward circumstances of your life might be. Truly, Jesus *is* the secret to your joy. Not family, not marriage, not your job, and not some kind of activity—golf, tennis, bridge, or whatever. Ultimate satisfaction can only be found in Jesus.

Solomon asked in Ecclesiastes 2:25: "For who can eat and who can have enjoyment without [God]?" The obvious answer is, no one. Enjoyment in life is rooted in Jesus. He's the source of it all, like a bubbling spring in the desert, flowing strong and pure, filled with light and joy. Paul could honestly say, "Yes, I'm a prisoner in Rome, chained between two guards day and night. And I certainly miss my friends in Jerusalem and Ephesus and Philippi and Antioch. But regardless of my circumstances, I have unspeakable joy. It has nothing to do with where I am or to whom I might be chained, but it has everything to do with the One who lives in me and whose life flows through me."

True Christianity

Jesus is the secret to overcoming your circumstances, and He wants to live His life through you. *That* is true Christianity. But so many people don't understand this. They think Christianity is a matter of sitting through a boring hour of someone reading a scripture and someone else delivering a lecture—and then trying to sing a song that sounds strange to the ears. And they find themselves looking at their watches and wondering, *How long until this drudgery is over?*

Make no mistake about it: that type of experience is *not* Christianity. It's not even close. Neither is Christianity gritting your teeth, trying hard to be like Jesus, and telling yourself, "I'm *going* to respond like Jesus in this situation. I'm *not* going to get mad or use profanity. I'm *not* going to get drunk this weekend. I'm going to *try hard*—so very hard—to be worthy of the Lord." That's not Christianity either. That's religion.

More than five hundred years ago, a German monk named Martin Luther took that route, and it left him feeling miserable, incomplete, guilty, and condemned. Luther had tried with everything within him to please God—fasting, praying, and doing incredibly painful acts of penance to gain favor with the Lord. Looking back later in life, he said of those days: "I lost touch with Christ, the Savior and Comforter, and made Him the jailer of my poor soul."[1]

Then, one day, Luther ran across a simple verse in the book of Romans that changed his life forever: "But the righteous man shall live by faith" (1:17).

You are not saved by your sweat; you are saved by His blood.

By faith? Not by trying hard? Not by sweating and gritting your teeth and abusing your body and straining to reach some kind of perfect standard? It is by *faith* . . . simple, childlike faith? Wow!

Everything changed for Luther when the truth of that one verse took hold in his heart. He suddenly understood that Christianity is not about "trying" at all. It's about trusting and believing God. It's about receiving the salvation that Jesus offers as a result of His death on the cross and resurrection from the tomb. It's about walking with Him by faith and letting Him live His life through a flawed but surrendered vessel. Yes, Christianity is the almighty Creator of the universe living His life through individual men and women, boys and girls. It's Jesus being real through the hearts and lives of His followers. *That* is Christianity.

Has the richness of Romans 1:17 gotten hold of your heart as it did Luther's? Or are you still trying to please Christ in your own strength and power? Remember this important spiritual truth: You are not saved by your sweat; you are saved by His blood. It is "not by works of righteousness which we have done, but according to His mercy he saved us" (Titus 3:5 KJV). Salvation comes when you put your little hand of faith into His great big hand of grace.

Furthermore, the Bible says, "As you therefore have received Christ Jesus the Lord, so walk in Him" (Col. 2:6 NKJV). You receive Christ by faith, and you walk with Him by faith. It's faith all the way. It has nothing to do with pushing yourself or trying in your flesh to live up to some perfect standard of righteousness. That's not what it's about. (I'm so glad . . . because the best of us can't even begin to measure up in our own strength.)

The Lord wants to live through you. And as He does, He becomes your personal source of satisfaction and contentment.

In the book *Extreme Devotion*, by the Voice of the Martyrs publishing group, I ran across the testimony of a Romanian pastor who had been imprisoned for his faith during that nation's dark, Communist past. In his writings, he reflected: "It is amazing how you can see Jesus in the face of other believers. Their faces shine, and it was quite an achievement for the glory of God to shine on the face of a Christian in Communist jails. We did not wash—I had not washed for three years—but the glory of God shone even from behind the crust of dirt. And they [the Christians in the prison] always had triumphant smiles on their faces."[2]

The Lord wants to live through you. And as He does, He becomes your personal source of satisfaction and contentment. In Him and Him alone "are hidden all the treasures of wisdom and knowledge" (Col. 2:3). Paul is telling us that if we tap into that Source, we can experience contentment flowing into our souls like water into an empty bottle. Tragically, multitudes of well-meaning people in our world attend church Sunday after Sunday and try so hard "to be good," but they have never experienced the awesome flow of God's presence and power.

But they *could*. And so can you.

Lesson #3: To Enjoy Contentment Regardless of the Circumstances, Put Your Faith into Practice.

You Can Make the Choice to Rejoice

Do you want to deal with your difficult circumstances and discontentment in a highly practical way? Then put your faith into practice, and make the choice to rejoice. In Philippians 4:4, Paul wrote, "Rejoice in the Lord always; again I will say, rejoice!" Paul made a conscious, definite decision to rejoice.

He could have easily looked at his imprisonment and his chains and his guards and said, "Man, this stinks. My life just rots in the sun. I wish God would put me out of my misery." But instead of grumbling and griping about his sorry state of affairs, he chose to rejoice and give thanks. And in making that important choice, as an act of his will, contentment became a reality in his life. Paul truly was a joyful, positive man with a hopeful outlook. No doubt, he would have been a pleasure to be around, given his genuine faith and contagious joy. In fact, members of Caesar's own household—soldiers and family members—were actually won to the Lord as they experienced firsthand his genuine faith and contagious joy, even in the midst of suffering (see Philippians 4:22).

Paul's choice to praise the Lord in his imprisonment wasn't without precedent. Years before, when he and his partner Silas came to Philippi for the very first time, they were falsely accused, seized by the authorities without a trial, savagely beaten and bloodied, and thrown into an inner prison, with their feet put in stocks. Make no mistake about it: this was an extremely painful, humiliating experience. "But about midnight," we learn, "Paul and Silas were praying and singing hymns of praise to God, and the prisoners were listening" (Acts 16:25).

Make the decision to rejoice first . . . and the emotions will follow after.

In the midst of pain and suffering, probably more than you and I have ever known, Paul was singing and praising God. He had made the choice to rejoice—not when it was easy, but when it was hard, extremely hard. That is precisely how to put your faith into practice, no matter what you may be dealing with today. Make the decision to rejoice first . . . and the emotions will follow after.

You Can Take Time to Pray

Be anxious for nothing, but in everything by prayer and supplication with thanksgiving let your request be made known to God.

Philippians 4:6

When you're overwhelmed, when you feel empty, when you wonder how you'll go on, it's time to pray. Often people struggling through difficulties don't realize—or they lose sight of the fact—that God is using those very circumstances to test them and strengthen their faith. They don't understand that this is the gymnasium of life, where they have a chance to see their weak and fragile faith grow steady and strong. God's grace in their lives will be enough—and more than enough—to meet their deepest needs, but they just don't get it.

As a result, if things don't change quickly, they become angry with God. Oftentimes, the unspoken prayer sounds something like this, *Well, forget it, God. Obviously, You don't care about my situation and what's happening to me, so I guess I'm on my own here. I'll just grab for all the happiness and fun I can get in life, because it doesn't matter, anyway. Walking with You just seems to make my life harder, not easier.*

The sad reality is, many people feel this way. They get bitter at God for things that have happened, and they walk away from the Lord.

One day, after Jesus had preached a particularly tough sermon, many of His onetime followers bailed on Him. Jesus watched sadly as the crowds turned their backs and walked away into the distance. Turning to look at Peter, James, John, and the rest of the disciples, Jesus said, "You do not want to leave, too, do you?"

Simon Peter spoke for the Twelve: "Lord, to whom shall we go? You have words of eternal life" (John 6:67–68).

Maybe at some point in your disappointment and pain, you have thought about walking away from Jesus. But where will you go? He is the Source, the Fountain, the Way, the Truth, and the Life. He is the Beginning and the End, and in Him are hidden all the treasures of wisdom and knowledge. In His presence is fullness of joy, and in His right hand there are pleasures forevermore (John 14:6; Rev. 22:13; Col. 2:3; Ps. 16:11). You're going to walk away from *that*? You're going to leave

Him, the One who is everything you need? Don't do it. Stay with the Lord, and keep pouring your heart out to Him. "Don't worry about anything; instead, pray about everything. Tell God what you need, and thank him for all he has done. If you do this, you will experience God's peace, which is far more wonderful than the human mind can understand. His peace will guard your hearts and minds as you live in Christ Jesus" (Phil. 4:6–7 NLT).

Keep going. Keeping praying.

YOU CAN DISCIPLINE YOUR MIND TO THINK CORRECTLY

Don't let your mind go south on you. When you experience those stuck-in-the-snowy-cul-de-sac moments, when you have those difficulties and setbacks come into your life—whether it's relational, financial, emotional, or health-related—it's easy to get negative, locking on to all the things that you fear, resent, and despise. It's like an airplane trapped in an ever-widening downward spiral. When your mind goes negative, your whole life gets negative, doesn't it? Why is that? Because as a man "thinks in his heart, so is he" (Prov. 23:7 NKJV).

So what solution did Paul give us in Philippians 4? He gave our minds a place to go—*a refuge*—when negative thoughts and emotions threaten to overwhelm us. He said, "Finally, brethren, whatever is true, whatever is honorable, whatever is right, whatever is pure, whatever is lovely, whatever is of good repute, if there is any excellence and if anything worthy of praise, [let your minds] dwell on these things" (v. 8). Paul didn't leave us up in the air as to what we should think about in such times; instead, he was very specific. Another translation puts it like this: "Fix your thoughts on what is true and good and right. Think about things that are pure and lovely, and dwell on the fine, good things in others. Think about all you can praise God for and be glad about" (LB).

The Bible talks about "taking every thought captive to the obedience of Christ" (2 Cor. 10:5). That means, don't let your thoughts bottom out in the gutter. Don't allow your mind to fill up with bitter contemplations, selfish desires, angry rants, or self-pity. Pull up those thoughts, just as an airplane pilot pulls on the stick to get out of a steep dive. Say to yourself, "Wait a minute. My sour, negative, faithless outlook on life right now is not honoring God; it's not praiseworthy. My feelings of discontentment are not telling me the truth or giving me the real score. Regardless of my circumstances, God is still God. He is still good and loving and all-powerful. I need to turn my thoughts back in the right direction." When your *out*-look is poor, that is the time to try the *up* look.

A Life-Changing Exercise

Dr. McDill, my friend and preaching professor, came to visit me in 2011. During the course of our conversation, I began sharing with him some of the things I'd been struggling with—some of the discontented areas of my life as a pastor.

He listened to me for a while, and then, in his direct, no-nonsense way, he said, "Jeff, let me tell you what you need to do."

"I'm all ears," I replied.

"I want you to do an exercise," he told me. "I want you to go home, take out a piece of paper, and write on the top of that paper, 'My situation and how I feel about it.' Then put those thoughts down, as honestly as you can. Write exactly what you feel. This is between you and God, and you're not going to share it with anyone else."

"Okay," I said.

"I'm serious," he went on. "Let it all out—all the frustration, disappointment, whatever. Then, when you're done, turn that paper over and on the other side write, 'But the truth is . . .' And then write about what this situation might look like from God's perspective. Write down what He may be trying to show you or accomplish in this situation that He has you walking through."

He went on to say, "Jeff, there are lots of guys who would trade your situation for their situation. You need to be grateful and thankful for what you have, and quit focusing on what you don't have."

Amazingly, when I sat down and did what Dr. McDill suggested, I began to see things in a totally different light . . . God's light.

I stopped griping and complaining about my adverse circumstances and started thanking God for where I was

When you're in the furnace of affliction, God's faithful, loving hand is on the thermostat. He controls the heat, and He has a purpose for your problems.

and what He was doing in me. In short, I ceased being an ingrate, focused on all the bad. I made the important choice to focus on the good things, to rejoice in the Lord and be truly grateful for all the undeserved blessings He had graciously bestowed upon me. And I thanked Him for the trials that He was using to help me grow. After engaging in McDill's little exercise, the alarm of discontentment stopped blaring . . . and the peace, joy, and happiness returned to my soul.

Perhaps you, too, need to engage in this important exercise. Trust me, it will change your outlook and your attitude. As you open your mind to see how God is involved in all that you're currently facing, and that He is orchestrating all of it for your good and His glory, it will remind you that when you're in the furnace of affliction, God's faithful, loving hand is on the thermostat. He controls the heat. He controls how long you're in it. He knows what's going on every second, and He really does work "all things . . . together for good to those who love God, to those who are called according to His purpose" (Rom. 8:28).

That's the truth . . . and it's the truth that changes everything.

In Philippians 1:12–18, Paul said, in essence, "God has used this whole prison experience to bring the gospel to even more people. And as other believers have seen my imprisonment, some of them have stepped into the gap. Now they're being empowered to share the gospel, too."

And how can you not love how he closed out the book in the second to the last verse? "All the saints greet you, *especially those of Caesar's household*" (4:22; emphasis added). Evidently, some of those soldiers to whom Paul had been chained ended up giving their lives to Jesus. Why? Because they saw that there was something real in Paul's life. He was joyful and contented—even in the midst of terrible circumstances. At some point, a number of those soldiers who saw him in prison must have said, "Hey, Paul, whatever you have, can you tell me about it? I want what you have. Can you share it with me?"

Are you in a situation that's causing you some discontentment? Think about this: You're probably not the only one who is aware of your difficult circumstances. There are others—more than you realize—who are looking on and wondering how you will respond. If you will yield to the Lord, if you will allow His life to radiate through yours, He will use that unwanted state of affairs in a way far beyond what you can imagine. He'll shine through you, as the sun shines through a break in the clouds on an overcast day. And maybe someone stumbling along on the highway to hell will notice that Son-burst and say, "What you have is real. I want that, too."

EIGHT

DEPRESSION

When All Hope Seems Lost

*Our days on the earth are like a shadow, and there is
no hope.*

1 CHRONICLES 29:15

*I'm alone Lord
alone
a thousand miles from home.
There's no one here who knows my name
except the clerk
and he spelled it wrong
no one to eat dinner with
laugh at my jokes
listen to my gripes
be happy with me about what happened today
and say that's great.
No one cares.
There's just this lousy bed
and slush in the street outside
between the buildings.
I feel sorry for myself
and I've plenty of reason
to. Maybe I ought to say
I'm on top of it
praise the Lord
things are great
but they're not.
Tonight
it's all
gray slush.[1]*

T he late Joe Bayly, Christian author and publishing executive, wrote that poem when he was away from home on a business trip, in the winter, and feeling lonely and blue. He called his poem "Psalm in a Hotel Room."

Was he depressed? Well, it's a good bet he was *that* night.

In some measure, we can all relate to the feelings Bayly expressed. From the Monday morning blues to full-blown clinical depression, most of us can say, "Yes, I have experienced some level of depression."

Depression is an emotional state of exaggerated feelings of sadness and intense discouragement that causes negative circumstances to overwhelm and debilitate a person's life.

Here's what's weird about depression. People can be depressed and not even realize it. They may sense that something's out of balance, something isn't quite right, but they don't know it's depression. A counselor friend of mine once told me, "Jeff, you'd be amazed at the scores of people who come in for counseling, thinking they have a problem in this area or that area . . . and what they find out is that their problem is really depression."

Depression has been vividly described as a black curtain of despair.

I talked to a friend who used to pastor a church in the city of Texarkana, Texas. "Jeff," he said, "I didn't realize it at the time, but when I was pastoring in Texarkana, I was extremely depressed. And it made my job so very difficult."

Could You Be Depressed?

Could that be your situation? Could you be depressed and not aware that it's your biggest problem? Perhaps you've felt that something is out of kilter in your life, but you don't know exactly what it is. Let me give you a few questions that will help you test yourself to see if, indeed, you might be wading a little in that dark swamp we call depression.

- Have you had a sudden weight loss or gain recently?
- Do you find yourself sleeping too much—or too little?
- Have you noticed a loss of interest in pleasurable activities?
- Are you experiencing fatigue or a lack of energy?
- Have you been overcome with feelings of hopelessness, worthlessness, uselessness, or helplessness?
- Do you have difficulty concentrating, remembering, or making decisions?
- Are you restless or irritable?
- Do you have thoughts of death or suicide?

If you answered yes to a number of these questions, it could very well be that you're suffering from depression and haven't even realized it.

You Are Not Alone

If you are dealing with depressive feelings right now, you need to know that you're in some very distinguished company. Numerous great and famous men and women throughout history have wrestled with that same troubling emotion we call depression.

Mark Twain struggled with depression. So did founding father John Adams, prime minister Winston Churchill, and even the reigning Queen of England, Elizabeth II. Charles Haddon Spurgeon, known in the 1800s as "the prince of preachers," wrestled with depression throughout the years of his long, fruitful pastorate. In fact, there would be weeks at a time when he would be out of the pulpit at the Metropolitan Tabernacle in London because he was too depressed to get up and preach. Spurgeon poignantly described his condition with these words of anguished revelation: "There are dungeons under the castles of despair."[2]

Numerous great and famous men and women throughout history have wrestled with depression.

In the book *Lectures to My Students*, Spurgeon wrote: "Fits of depression come over most of us. Usually cheerful as we may be, we must at intervals be cast down. The strong are not always vigorous, the wise are not always ready, the brave are not always courageous, and the joyous are not always happy. There may be here and there men of iron . . . but surely the rust frets even these."[3]

One Midwestern lawyer who lived in the 1800s had so much difficulty with depression that concerned friends removed all the knives out of his house, in fear that he might kill himself. At one point this troubled man wrote, "I am now the most miserable man living. Whether I shall ever be better, I cannot tell. I am afraid I shall not."[4]

But he did get better. Much better. And he went on to become the sixteenth president of the United States of America—Abraham Lincoln.

Many prominent people have endured episodes of depression . . . and have emerged from those dark tunnels to accomplish great things in their lives—or become mighty servants of the living God. Let me throw one more name out there to show you what I mean.

Elijah the prophet.

GOOD CHAPTER, BAD CHAPTER

We can all look back on what we might call great chapters in our lives. For Elijah, that chapter was recorded in Scripture in 1 Kings 18.

Talk about a literal mountaintop experience! In this portion of Scripture, Elijah had a face-off on the peak of Mount Carmel, with 450 prophets of the false god Baal, along with 400 more prophets of Asherah, Baal's female counterpart. This was like a "Super Bowl" for the people of Israel. Hundreds, perhaps even thousands, gathered to see this "Battle of the Gods."

In essence, Elijah had thrown out this challenge: "Let's stop messing around, and let's find out who is really God. If Yahweh, the God of Israel, is God, let's serve Him. But if Baal is god, then let's serve him. How long are we going to straddle the fence? How long will we hesitate between the two opinions? Let's decide—here, today—who is God and let's follow *that* God!"

The people thought that sounded good, so the contest began. It would shape up like this: The prophets of Baal would place an animal sacrifice on the altar and then call on their god to send fire down to consume it. Then Elijah, the sole prophet of God, would do the same. And everyone had agreed: The deity who answered by fire would be declared the true and living God of Israel.

If Elijah was worried about the contest, it certainly didn't show. He even gave the prophets of Baal "home field advantage" (or so they thought). Those who worshiped false gods thought that the higher in elevation you were, the closer you were to the gods. So they all liked worshiping on high places or mountaintops. "Okay," Elijah said. "We'll do this on the top of Mount Carmel." And if numbers meant anything, Elijah was putting himself at a distinct disadvantage: 850 versus 1.

From 9:00 a.m. to noon, the prophets of Baal cried out to their god. But alas, he didn't answer. Elijah even started to make fun of them, taunting them to pray louder because their god must be asleep, or on vacation . . . or on the toilet (see 1 Kings 18:27 CEV). So they shouted louder and cut themselves until the blood flowed to show Baal their sincerity, commitment, and sacrifice. Baal, however, did not respond. How could he, since he never existed in the first place? He was a *false* god.

At 3:00 p.m., it was Elijah's turn. He built the altar with twelve stones, symbolizing the twelve tribes of Israel. Next he placed the wood and the oxen on the altar. Then, in order to up the ante, he had the altar doused with water—not once, not twice, but three times. Everything was drenched, and there were five gallons of standing water in a trench all around the sacrifice. Then Elijah called upon Yahweh God, the almighty King of the universe. He called upon Him once . . . and that was all that was needed. God answered immediately by raining fire down from heaven, totally consuming the sacrifice, the water, *and* the twelve stones of the altar. Game over. Total wipeout.

When the people saw how God had responded, they cried out, "The LORD, He is God; the LORD, He is God" (v. 39). Wow, what a moment for the prophet! What an awesome display of God's presence, power, and sovereignty. Elijah immediately had all the false prophets seized, and he put them to death by the brook Kishon.

It had been an amazing, crushing victory, the kind that changes everything for good and for God. Elijah must have thought to himself, *This is the tipping point. This will turn everything around in Israel. All the idol worship will be gone, and even Ahab, our wicked king, and Jezebel, his worthless, evil wife, will finally turn their hearts to the Lord God. How exciting that I would live to see this. Hallelujah!*

But his victory *didn't* turn things around. Revival didn't break out as he had figured it would. As a matter of fact, rather than being hailed as a hero for bringing back the worship of the true and living God to Israel, Elijah suddenly found himself Public Enemy Number One and under an imminent death threat. The prophets of Baal may have been history, but it really made no difference. Ahab, Jezebel, and Israel weren't about to turn back to God.

If 1 Kings 18 had been the greatest experience in Elijah's ministry, 1 Kings 19 was the lowest point, marking the prophet's incredible slide from a mountaintop of elation into the darkest valley of his life. Here's how it all plays out in Scripture:

> Now Ahab told Jezebel all that Elijah had done, and how he had killed all the prophets with the sword. Then Jezebel sent a messenger to Elijah, saying, "So may the gods do to me and even more, if I do not make your life as the life of one of them by tomorrow about this time." And he was afraid and arose and ran for his life and came to Beersheba, which belongs to Judah, and left his servant there. But he himself went a day's journey into the wilderness, and came and sat down under a juniper tree; and he

requested for himself that he might die, and said, "It is enough; now, O LORD, take my life, for I am not better than my fathers." (vv. 1–4)

Was he depressed? You'd better believe it. He was so down in the dumps that he wanted to die. In exhaustion, despair, and disillusionment, he begged God to take his life.

As far as Elijah was concerned, it was the end of everything. As far as God was concerned, it was a new beginning.

GOD'S MESSAGE IN DEPRESSION

Elijah, one of God's choice servants in that day, was depressed, very depressed. But he would soon find out that God had a message for him in and through his depression—and that hope was about to break through the prophet's gloom and despair.

As demonstrated throughout this book, God uses our over-the-top negative emotions like a smoke alarm, to get our attention and to wake us up to the fact that there's a fire ablaze in our lives.

When it comes to the blaring smoke alarm of depression, locating the fire isn't always that easy. Those deep feelings of sadness

> *Elijah, one of God's choice servants in that day, was depressed, very depressed. But he would soon find out that God had a message for him in and through his depression—and that hope was about to break through the prophet's gloom and despair.*

and lethargy may come from any number of different directions —or all of them at once.

That's how it was for Elijah. In fact, God was dealing with His prophet in four specific areas of his life. As it happens, those are the same four areas we need to check out in our lives when we feel that heavy blanket of depression beginning to drape itself over us, smothering our peace, joy, and zest for life.

EMOTION: Depression
WARNING: Your God-given sense of hope is on fire.

1. WHEN YOU FEEL DEPRESSED, CHECK YOUR PHYSICAL CONDITION.

> [Elijah] lay down and slept under a juniper tree; and, behold, there was an angel touching him, and he said to him, "Arise, eat." Then he looked and, behold, there was at his head a bread cake baked on hot stones, and a jar of water. So he ate and drank and lay down again. The angel of the LORD came again a second time and touched him and said, "Arise, eat, because the journey is too great for you." So he arose and ate and drank and went in the strength of that food forty days and forty nights to Horeb, the mountain of God. (1 Kings 19:5–8)

Depressed Elijah was totally worn out. He was physically and emotionally exhausted. He'd just come off the highest, most amazing experience of his life, and then in a matter of mere hours, he'd slid all the way to the bottom.

Rock bottom. From the highest high to the lowest low, just like that, he was now in the dungeon of despair, and he wanted to die . . . he prayed to die.

Did you know that depression often hits when you've had some exciting, defining, mountaintop experience with the Lord? Oftentimes right on the heels of some marvelous, memorable high point comes a big drop-off—and you feel a thousand miles away from where you had just been. Why does that happen? Because, as Peter tells us, "your adversary, the devil, prowls around like a roaring lion, seeking someone to devour" (1 Peter 5:8). Sometimes when we're relaxed, elated, and jubilant, we let our spiritual guard down, forget to be careful, and lose sight of the fact that spiritual warfare is a 24/7 reality. When Satan sees us in a vulnerable moment, he pounces, anxious to steal our victory and rob us of our joy.

If Satan can't rob us of our salvation, he will do all he can to steal every bit of joy out of that salvation while we remain on earth.

If Satan can't rob us of our salvation, he will do all he can to steal every bit of joy out of that salvation while we remain on earth. That's what happened to Elijah, and it happened when he was very, very tired.

How did he get so tired? To understand his exhaustion, we need to back up and see exactly what transpired between the Mount Carmel victory and the southern wilderness prayer for death.

Leaving Mount Carmel, the scene of God's great victory, he *ran* all the way to Jezreel, the royal residence city of the king and queen. That little jaunt was just a few miles short of a marathon. What's more, the Bible tells us that he outran King Ahab as he rode in his chariot. To say the least, Elijah was moving fast to get to the revival that he thought was sure to sweep through Jezreel.

But there was to be no revival, no victory party in Jezreel. While he was there, Queen Jezebel sent him a message that rained on his parade big-time: "So you killed all my prophets, huh? You're toast, Elijah. We're getting ready to stick a fork in you. By this time tomorrow, you'll be as dead as they are."

So, Ahab and Jezebel weren't going to turn to the Lord, after all. There would be no national revival. In fact, they were going to kill Elijah! All of a sudden, Elijah's great victory on the mountaintop seemed to turn to ashes in his hands. Filled with fear for his life, the prophet took off running again, this time all the way down south to Beersheba.

That's about 100 miles.

From there, he left his servant (who must have been as tired as Elijah) and headed a full day's journey into the wilderness—another 15 miles or so. When he finally crawled under that humble juniper tree, he'd traveled about 140 miles. On foot.

Without question, Elijah was totally spent and beyond exhausted.

So what did God do when He met him under that tree? Did He give him a lecture? Did He question His faith and chide him for his fear and depression? Did He demand that Elijah give an account of himself? No. Do you know what God did? He gave His weary, fearful prophet much-needed sleep and refreshment. First, He let him rest. Then He sent an angel to fix Elijah a snack of hot, fresh bread and cool, clear water. After the prophet slept some more, the angel woke him up again and said, "Get up and eat some more, for there is a long journey ahead of you" (1 Kings 19:7 TLB).

Let's face it: Physical exhaustion and depletion are often key factors in the malady called depression.

Vince Lombardi, the legendary football coach of the Green Bay Packers, once reportedly said, "Fatigue makes cowards of us all."

Vince Lombardi, the legendary football coach of the Green Bay Packers, once reportedly said, "Fatigue makes cowards of us all."

God dealt with Elijah's physical fatigue first, and that's also the first thing you should look at when you find depression beginning to dog your steps like an unwanted shadow. Are you getting sufficient rest, relaxation, and refreshment? How important is that? It's so important that God put it in the Ten Commandments. The fourth commandment says: "Six days you shall labor and do all your work, but the seventh is a sabbath of the LORD your God; in it you shall not do any work" (Ex. 20:9–10).

The Sabbath is a day for no work. It's a day to rest. God builds into every week a vacation day when He says, *"Listen, I want you to put your work down today. I want you to rest, relax, and recharge your batteries one day each week."* But we so often blow off that commandment and keep pushing ahead, trying to do more and more and more.

In his insightful book, *Leading on Empty*, Pastor Wayne Cordeiro relates a story of going for a jog one evening while he was in California for a speaking engagement. Cordeiro wrote: "One minute I was jogging along on the sidewalk, and the next minute I was sitting on a curb, sobbing uncontrollably. I couldn't stop, and I didn't have a clue what was happening to me."

Something inside him had snapped. He went on to describe how he had used up all his emotional and physical resources. He wasn't even running on fumes anymore; there was nothing, absolutely nothing, left in his tank. Cordeiro then explained how many pastors and leaders follow that same path. Used up and burned-out on the inside, they continue to lead on empty. "If you keep doing that," Cordeiro insisted, "if you keep running the engine on the red line, eventually something's going to blow."[5]

Jesus would have agreed. In Mark 6:31, after an intense period of ministry, He said to His disciples, "Come away by yourselves to a secluded place and rest a while." Mark went on to explain that "there were many people coming and going, and they did not even have time to eat."

The King James Version translates Mark 6:31 this way: "Come ye yourselves apart into a desert place, and rest a while." I like that wording because it is so poignantly descriptive. If you don't take the time to come apart and rest, you *will* come apart . . . at the seams! You'll disintegrate emotionally, as Wayne Cordeiro did on the curb of that busy California street.

Am I speaking to myself in this chapter? Yes, I am! I haven't been very good at allowing time for rest and refreshment in my schedule because it always seems that there's more to do than I could ever get done. There are so many needs. But what I've had to learn is that every need doesn't equal a call on my life. There will always be needs, but God wants me to respond to the ones that He specifically lays on my heart. So I say to Him every morning, "Lord, what needs do You want to meet through me this day?" He will have to help me pick and choose and delegate, because I can't meet every need. Only the Lord can do that.

How Is *Your* Physical Health?

How sure are you that you're physically healthy? Have you been to the doctor for a checkup? Sometimes, lingering depression can have purely physical sources—perhaps a chemical imbalance in the body. If that's the case, there may be some medicine you could take to bring proper balance back. It doesn't necessarily mean you have to take it forever; maybe you can take it for a time and receive some needed help to get you through a particularly rough patch of life. If you are depressed and don't know why, don't hesitate to talk to your doctor about it. Your current physical condition may be a major factor.

2. When you feel depressed, check your spiritual condition.

> Then he came there to a cave and lodged there; and behold, the word of the Lord came to him, and He said to him, "What are you doing here, Elijah?" He said, "I have been very zealous for the Lord, the God of hosts; for the sons of Israel have forsaken Your covenant, torn down Your altars and killed Your prophets with the sword. And I alone am left; and they seek my life, to take it away."
>
> So He said, "Go forth and stand on the mountain before the Lord." And behold, the Lord was passing by! And a great and strong wind was rending the mountains and breaking in pieces the rocks before the Lord; but the Lord was not in the wind. And after the wind an earthquake, but the Lord was not in the earthquake. After the earthquake a fire, but the Lord was not in the fire; and after the fire a sound of a gentle blowing. When Elijah heard it, he wrapped his face in his mantle and went out and stood in the entrance of the cave. And behold, a voice came to him and said, "What are you doing here, Elijah?" (1 Kings 19:9–13)

After dealing with His servant's physical needs, God moved on to his spiritual needs. Twice, He asked Elijah the same question: "What are you doing here, Elijah?"

As you read his story in the Bible, one thing is very clear: Elijah had always been led by the Lord.

- In 1 Kings 17, the Lord led him to deliver a word of judgment to King Ahab, and he did.
- Then the Lord led him to a hideout in the desert, where he would drink from a brook and be fed by the ravens.
- After that, the Lord led him to a widow in Zarephath whom God had instructed to provide for him.
- Next, God led him back to Ahab, where Elijah issued the challenge to those prophets of Baal.
- Finally, "the hand of the LORD" guided him back to Jezreel (1 Kings 18:46).

Again and again, he was led by the Lord. Yet when he got that note from Jezebel, he panicked and—without waiting for a word from heaven—started running south like a frightened jackrabbit. In that moment, he wasn't led by the Lord; he was led by fear.

He had no command to go a hundred miles from Jezreel to Beersheba, nor to go two hundred miles from Beersheba to Mount Horeb. In essence, he ended up three hundred miles off course. No wonder God asked him, *"What are you doing* here, *Elijah?"*

When Elijah began running from Jezebel, he wasn't being led by the Lord; he was being led by fear.

Here's a question for you: In your fear or anxiety or depression, is it possible that you have put distance between yourself and God? In other words, are you in the wrong place?

The Tragedy of Getting Away from God

Remember the story Jesus told in Luke 15 about the prodigal son who left his father for the glitz and glamour of "the far country"? That boy wound up broke, uncared for, working in a pigsty, longing to eat pig slop in the hopes that it would ease his intense hunger pangs. Without question, the prodigal was in the wrong place . . . until he finally "came to his senses" and came home.

A lady I know walked away from her husband and family to pursue a relationship with another man. Although she claims to be a Christian, she said, "I'm tired of listening to God. I'm tired of doing what God wants me to do. I want to do what *I* want to do." Like the prodigal son, she set out for the thrills and chills of the far country. But the far country only leads to the pigsty.

Did she end up in the wrong place? Yes, she did.

The book of Proverbs tells us, "There is a way which seems right to a man, but its end is the way of death" (16:25).

Are you in the wrong place, spiritually? The fact is, if you're not in the right place, if you're out of position, you won't experience the joy of God. The Bible tells us, "In His presence is fullness of joy" (Ps. 16:11). In contrast, the Bible says, "The rebellious dwell in a parched land" (Ps. 68:6).

Furthermore, are you obsessed with your problems and the obstacles in your path, or are you focused on the God who is a zillion times greater than all the problems and obstacles you could ever face?

Depressed people are fixated on the wrong things. Like Elijah, they have taken their eyes off the Lord and focused on the curses and threats of Jezebel. If you focus your eyes on and fill your mind with all the negative circumstances that swirl around you, those adversities will simply overwhelm you.

You need to get your eyes—and ears—back on God.

You Need to See Him . . . and Hear Him

Earlier, we looked at the passage where God invited Elijah to go up to the mountain, because He was going to pass by him.

While we want God to speak to us in big, miraculous ways, more often than not He chooses to speak through a gentle blowing . . . a still, small voice.

You will recall that a mighty wind came; then an earthquake; and then a scorching fire. But the Lord wasn't in any of these. He showed up as a "gentle blowing."

But you and I prefer the earthquake and the fire, don't we? We're looking for God in the big events, the dramatic encounters, the amazing miracles. We say, "Do something miraculous, God! Come down into my life with a blast and a blaze! Shake this place, and shake all these difficulties out of my life."

Yes, He will do that sometimes. More often than not, however, He chooses to speak into our lives just as He did to Elijah: through a gentle blowing . . . a still, small voice. Why do you think God chooses to speak that way? I mean, wouldn't it be more helpful if He shouted it out so we were sure to hear Him? Let's think about that for a moment.

It's easy to hear when someone is shouting, isn't it? But if God is speaking in a whisper, you have to quiet down to hear Him. You have to really listen. If you never quiet your heart before the Lord, if you never get away to a solitary place or a quiet room, you may not hear Him. And you may miss what He has to say to you. The reason God doesn't often shout is because He speaks to those who really want to hear, who will turn off the noise and open their ears.

Most of us live in a noisy world, don't we? We're used to hearing a buzz of traffic, airplanes, music, TV, barking dogs, chirping cell phones, and all sorts of activity around us. Even when we're on the treadmill or walking around the block, we stick little earbuds in our ears to keep the music going.

You have to get away from the noise to hear God speak. You have to get close to Him to hear His whisper. And whatever you have to do to hear God speak is always well worth it, because His words are life!

THE MEDICINE OF PRAISE

Could it be that you're not listening to the Lord and have become focused on the wrong things? Are you forgetting to praise Him? Depressed people often do. They mope around the house, and everything is a struggle and a chore. Do you hear praises coming from their lips? Not hardly. They are too filled with gloom and doom to praise the Lord. *But praise is the very thing they desperately need to do.*

Did you know that giving praise to God is one of the greatest weapons against depression? The fact is, our enemy, the devil, thrives in the darkness. And depressed people will sit inside a dark house with the curtains drawn and the lights down low.

Did you know that giving praise to God is one of the greatest weapons against depression?

How do you turn on the light? How do you brighten up your soul? You do it with praise, because God inhabits the praises of His people (see Psalm 22:3). You quit moaning, you quit groaning, and you begin to praise the Lord for who He is and what He has done. The psalmist said, "Seven times a day I praise You" (Ps. 119:164). Hebrews 13:15 tells us, "Let us continually offer up a sacrifice of praise to God, that is, the fruit of lips that give thanks to His name."

When David was on the run from King Saul, that jealous, psycho king who wanted to track him down and kill him, David fought with the giant of depression. Yet David won . . . and his knockout punch was praise. He wrote: "I will bless the LORD at all times; His praise shall continually be in my mouth" (Ps. 34:1). Praising God *continually*. What a powerful antidote to the black darkness known as depression.

"Ah," you say, "but I'm just too depressed to praise God. I just don't have the energy." Oh, yes you do, because God Himself will give it to you. Isaiah 40:29 says, "He energizes those who get tired, gives fresh strength to dropouts" (*The Message*). By faith open your mouth, move your vocal cords, and begin to declare the wonders of who He is. Start thanking Him and blessing Him for being alive in your life and for giving you ample strength to deal with your life situation, whatever it may be. As you begin to praise, the energy will come.

Sometimes, being a pastor can be especially tough. Occasionally, things happen that cause pastors to fall out of favor with some of the people. I can identify with the beleaguered minister who said, "My greatest challenge at my church is keeping the 50 percent of the congregation who don't like me away from the 50 percent who are not sure." Obviously just a joke, but it can sure feel like the truth at times.

One time in my ministry, I had a season where I was not everyone's "favorite pastor." More and more people were clicking on the box "not a fan." Church attendance and offerings started to take a hit, and many unfavorable and untrue things were being said about me around the church and the community. Some friends turned on me to such an extent that it seemingly became their mission to see me fired. It was not a fun time for Debbie and me. We could feel the black darkness of depression setting in as more and more people left the church.

I wish we could say we rose above all the negatives and let them harmlessly fall to the ground like water off a duck's back, but that wouldn't be true. The things that were said and done were painful, and depression began to seep into our hearts and our home.

What was there to do? Start practicing what I had been preaching.

Debbie and I made a conscious choice to play songs of praise from Christian radio day and night in our home. In less than a week, the mood shifted from discouragement and despair to joy and excitement over what God was getting ready to do. The praise music got us to focus our eyes on the Lord and His great and wonderful promises for us and for the church.

It was one simple thing: playing praise music 24/7 . . . but it made all the difference in the world.

Are you feeling depressed? Check your spiritual condition. Check to see if you are where you're supposed to be and if you are remembering to praise Him.

3. When you feel depressed, check your mental condition.

What kind of thoughts are you allowing to fill your mind? That question is so crucial.

Elijah had developed something of a martyr complex, convincing himself that he was "the only one left" in Israel who remained faithful to God. In the space of just four verses, Elijah told the Lord twice, "I alone am left; and they seek my life, to take it away" (1 Kings 19:10, 14).

I'm the only one left, Lord.
Everyone has turned against You.

I'm no better than my fathers.

I've tried and tried, but I've failed.

Take my life God. Just stick a fork in me; I'm done.

(vv. 4, 10, paraphrased)

There was only one problem with these comments from Elijah: they weren't true! God wasn't finished with him. He had more important work for the prophet to accomplish in the days to come. In addition, there were more true believers in Israel than Elijah had even dreamed. God said, "Yet I reserve seven thousand in Israel—all whose knees have not bowed down to Baal and all whose mouths have not kissed him" (v. 18 NIV).

You can't allow yourself to dwell on lies. If you do, Satan, the father of lies, will keep you supplied with a steady stream of them!

"I alone am left" was not even in the ballpark of truth.

What is the point here for you? You can't allow yourself to dwell on lies. If you do, Satan, the father of lies, will keep you supplied with a steady stream of them!

BUT IT SURELY *FEELS* LIKE THE TRUTH

Why do negative thoughts and lies seem so credible to us so much of the time? Because they match our *feelings.* Elijah *felt* that he was the lone believer. He *thought* that was the truth. But feelings are often false. Emotions simply aren't a reliable barometer of the truth. A pilot flying in a terrible storm had better not rely on what "feels right" to him. He had better rely on his instruments if he wants to make it through without crashing.

Faith is related to spiritual facts, to biblical reality. We can't "feel" our way to faith. We have to take our stand on the facts of God's Word and let our feelings follow when (or if) they will.

Jesus said, "If you hold to my teaching, you are really my disciples. Then you will know the truth, and the truth will set you free" (John 8:32 NIV). In other words, we need to walk in the truth, fill our minds with it, and hold to it, even when our feelings and the circumstances around us seem to be shouting another message. "That," says Jesus, "is the way to true freedom."

MEDITATING ON THE TRUTHS OF GOD'S WORD

What are some of the truths you need to have locked away in your heart? There are literally hundreds of them! But how about these critical ones for starters:

"YOU ARE NOT HOPELESS."

One of the key characteristics of depression is a sense of hopelessness. Depressed people feel that nothing is ever going to get better, and their lives really don't matter. But, the Word of God says otherwise: "'I know the plans that I have for you,' declares the LORD, 'plans for welfare and not for calamity to give you a future and a hope'" (Jer. 29:11). Romans 15:13 says, "Now may the God of hope fill you with all joy and peace in believing so that you will abound in hope by the power of the Holy Spirit."

I love the fact that God is the God of hope . . . and He wants to fill your heart with hope this day, and fill it to overflowing. Whatever you are facing—injury, disease,

I love the fact that God is the God of hope . . . and He wants to fill your heart with hope this day, and fill it to overflowing.

divorce, loss, or financial ruin—it's not over for you. If Jesus can raise Lazarus from the grave, He can do a miracle in you, regardless of your circumstances.

"You are not a loser or a failure."

Years ago, when I worked in the chemical business, I had a customer with a big tattoo on his arm that read, "Born to Lose." I was stunned. I remember thinking to myself, *What? Were they running a special at the tattoo parlor? Was this tattoo free?* Who in his right mind would tattoo "Born to Lose" on his arm? And then it hit me. The reason he tattooed that phrase on his arm is because it was already tattooed on his brain.

Is is tattooed on your brain?

The sad truth is, there are many people who see themselves as nothing more than a no-good, miserable loser. Their negative self-talk goes something like this: *Who am I kidding? I'm not going to succeed here. I can't rise above. I can't overcome. I am going to fail, just like always. It's just not in the cards for me.* The "Born to Lose" tattoo strikes again.

We used to have a little dog named Max. He was part Chihuahua, part dachshund—known officially to dog breeders as a Chiweenie. (I am not kidding. Look it up.) My daughter Sarah always used to call Max "Loser." It would make her mother so mad. Debbie would say, "Don't call Max a loser. It will affect his self-esteem!"

One day, Sarah took a magic marker and drew a big *L* on poor Max's head. It was there for several weeks because she wrote it in permanent ink that wouldn't wash off! I'm sure our other dog made fun of him when we weren't around because he had that big, dark *L* on his head for so long.

Maybe at some point in your life someone did to you what

Sarah did to Max. The individual may not have used a marking pen on your forehead, but he or she spoke harshly to you, criticized you, made fun of you, and led you to believe you were just a zero and a loser.

I am here to tell you . . . *that's a lie!* And don't let that lie linger in your brain for one minute longer. Romans 8:37 tells us: "But in all these things we overwhelmingly conquer through Him who loved us." We are *super* conquerors (*hupernikao* in the Greek) through Christ. Every Christian is part of the winning team, not the losing team. If you are joined with Jesus Christ, you're joined to the greatest winner in the universe.

You say you've failed? Join the club. We all have failed. But that doesn't make you a *failure*. If you'll let Him, God will enable you to get back on your feet and keep moving forward. Proverbs 24:16 declares: "A righteous man falls seven times, and rises again." I don't care what you've done or what has happened, it's time for you to get up and get back in the game.

"YOU ARE NOT UNLOVED, UNACCEPTED, AND ALL ALONE."

Elijah felt 100 percent isolated and despised, because that's what his immediate circumstances and his feelings kept telling him . . . but he was believing a lie. And so are you, if you fall for it! Ephesians 1:6 says you are "accepted in the Beloved" (NKJV). In other words, if you know Jesus Christ as Savior and Lord, God the Father accepts you. On what basis? Your good works, good name, and good character? Heavens, no! He doesn't accept you because of you. He accepts you because of Jesus.

In John 17, Jesus prayed His awesome, high priestly prayer. In that prayer, He said something totally amazing: "I in them and You in Me, that they may be perfected in unity, so that the world may know that You sent Me, *and loved them, even as You have loved Me*" (v. 23; emphasis added).

If God the Father loves you as much as He loves Jesus the Son, how could you ever believe that you are unloved?

Wait a minute. Did you read that right? God loves you as much as He loves His own Son? Could it be? God's Word says it's so. If God the Father loves you as much as He loves Jesus the Son, how could you ever believe that you are unloved?

Are you all alone? No! In Hebrews 13:5, God tells us, "I will never desert you, nor will I ever forsake you."

What's the bottom line here? You and I must combat the devil's lies with God's unchanging truth. If we are to experience victory of the darkness of depression, we must cling to His promises like a bulldog with a T-bone steak.

4. WHEN YOU FEEL DEPRESSED, CHECK YOUR FOCUS.

Even though he was one of the greatest men of faith and courage in all of Scripture, Elijah had become very self-centered by the time he was visited by God in the wilderness. The truth is, all depressed people become self-centered. Elijah was having a little pity party in 1 Kings 19 because he was alone and listening to his own dark thoughts.

The Lord, however, knew just what to do. He gave him an assignment, and it involved anointing other people for specific and important positions.

Then the LORD told him, "Go back the way you came, and travel to the wilderness of Damascus. When you arrive there, anoint

Hazael to be king of Aram. Then anoint Jehu grandson of Nimshi to be king of Israel, and anoint Elisha son of Shaphat from the town of Abel-meholah to replace you as my prophet." (1 Kings 19:15–16 NLT)

Elijah had prayed to die, but God didn't answer that prayer. In fact, Elijah would end up being one of only two men in the Bible who never died. (Enoch was the other.) God took Him to heaven alive, in a whirlwind and a chariot of fire. Before that time came, however, God still had significant work for him to do.

By directing Elijah to anoint Elisha as his successor, God was not only helping Elijah to locate his future replacement; He was also bringing him a much-needed friend and companion.

It was as if God were saying to him, *"Quit thinking about yourself, Elijah. Quit sitting in your room all by yourself, just contemplating how lonely you are and how bad life has become. Get out there and engage! Get your eyes off yourself and start helping other people. Follow My plan, and I will even bring you a friend to share your burden and lighten your load."*

That was God's plan for Elijah's depression. The prophet needed to engage with others, and he needed to give. Meanwhile, a young prophet-in-the-making, named Elisha, needed a mentor and a guide.

> *That was God's plan for Elijah's depression. The prophet needed to engage with others, and he needed to give.*

Paul wrote: "Carry each other's burdens, and in this way you will fulfill the law of Christ" (Gal. 6:2 NIV).

Admittedly, the idea of giving something when you're depressed seems like a daunting challenge. How can you give when you feel you have nothing inside? My friend Larry lost his wife to cancer.

He was so broken he couldn't even talk without crying. But then he met an older man in his church, named Joe, whose wife had just been diagnosed with that same disease. The Lord led Larry to call Joe several times; he sympathized with him, prayed for him, and even cried with him. Later, Joe revealed that no one had helped him through that dark valley as much as Larry had.

Do what you can, even if it doesn't seem like much. Take a plate of cookies to the neighbor next door. Reach out of your isolation and, with God's enabling, seek to make a difference in someone's life. Minister to other people. "Give," as Jesus said, "and it will given to you" (Luke 6:38).

Dr. Karl Menninger was once asked what advice he would give a person who felt the onset of depression. The famed psychiatrist answered, "Lock up your house, go across the railroad tracks, find someone in need and do something for them."[6]

Elijah went on to accomplish great things for God, but his young pupil and companion, Elisha, did even greater exploits than his teacher. In obedience to the Lord, the older man gave out of his emptiness, and the younger man ended up with a double portion of his spirit.

That's the math of heaven, and it doesn't always add up on an earthly calculator. But that's okay. You can experience it even if you never understand it.

CONCLUSION

The Choice Is Yours

*I call heaven and earth to witness against you today, that
I have set before you life and death, the blessing and the
curse. So choose life in order that you may live.*

DEUTERONOMY 30:19

I heard about a man who got a flat tire right outside an asylum. As he pulled over to change the tire, a mental patient began to watch him through the fence.

The man jacked up the car, took off the lug nuts, and carefully placed them inside the hubcap. But, as circumstances would have it, the crowbar inadvertently hit the hubcap, and all four lug nuts flew into the storm sewer. The man was frustrated and flabbergasted. In desperation, he exclaimed, "What am I going to do now!?"

The mental patient who was watching him offered this piece of sage advice: "Hey mister, why don't you take one lug nut off the other three tires? You can easily ride with three lug nuts in place on each tire until you can get to a garage and get the lost lug nuts replaced."

The man thought for a moment and said, "Why, that is a great idea! Thank you. Say, what is a sharp guy like you doing in a place like this, anyway?"

The patient answered, "I'm in here because I'm crazy, not stupid."

As we come to the close of our look at the negative emotions of inferiority, anger, loneliness, guilt, discontentment, anxiety, frustration, and depression, let me encourage you. If you are struggling with some or all of these unwanted feelings, you are neither crazy *nor* stupid. What you are is human. Everyone battles these emotions to one degree or another.

The good news is God doesn't want any of us to get stuck in one or more of these troubling feelings. He wants us to let our internal smoke alarms help us find the real fire so we can douse the flames and get things right inside. God is a good God who wants His love, joy, peace, and power to reign in our hearts.

IT'S A CHOICE

One of my favorite passages in the Bible is found in the closing verses of Luke 10, the story of Mary, Martha, and Jesus, which we discussed earlier. In this little story, the Lord paints a vivid picture of two lives you and I can choose to live. The first one is a life filled with worry, frustration, anger, and inner turmoil. The second is a life filled with sweet peace and great joy:

> Now as [Jesus and His disciples] were traveling along, He entered a certain village; and a woman named Martha welcomed Him into her home. She had a sister called Mary, who was seated at the Lord's feet, listening to His word. But Martha was distracted with all her preparations; and she came up to Him and said, "Lord, do You not care that my sister has left me to do all the serving alone? Then tell her to help me." But the Lord answered and said to her, "Martha, Martha, you are worried and bothered about so many things; but only one thing is necessary, for Mary has chosen the good part, which shall not be taken away from her." (vv. 38–42)

The sisters were having Jesus over to the house for Sunday dinner. Martha wanted everything to be perfect: the rolls, the mashed potatoes, the corn casserole, the salad, the pecan pie, and of course, the main dish—Martha's Meatloaf. I can just hear the excitement in her voice as she whispered to herself, "I'm making my famous meatloaf for the Master."

But a perfect meatloaf for the perfect Master required lots of work, so much so that she missed spending time with the Master as she was busy in the kitchen. She needed Mary's help . . . but Mary was nowhere to be found. She had left the kitchen and entered the den. She was enjoying the Master and neglecting the meatloaf. And Martha was not happy about it!

When she saw Mary at Jesus' feet, soaking up His words, no doubt she said under her breath, "Doesn't Mary know what's really important here? It's the meatloaf!"

Mary did know what was really important . . . and it *wasn't* the meatloaf.

When Martha came out of the kitchen, she was fit to be tied. The smoke alarm was blaring BIG-time, but she had not a clue where the real fire was. She was frustrated, angry, resentful, anxious, and discontented all at the same time. She was so upset with her sister that she starting giving orders to Jesus! "Lord, if You care about me and the great injustice I am experiencing right now, then tell Mary to help me!" Martha exclaimed. (You can know for certain that you have derailed somewhere along the line when you start giving orders to Jesus.)

I just love the way Jesus answered her. Allow me to paraphrase a little to get the full import of His words. I can just hear the compassion in His voice as He repeated her name for loving emphasis. *"Martha, Martha, my dear girl, you are worried and bothered and upset about so many things . . . things that really don't matter. You have allowed your meatloaf dinner to take center stage, and you've missed the real issue here: spending time with Me. Mary made the right choice to leave the kitchen and the truly insignificant cares of the meal, and sit at My feet. I'm not going to tell her to leave; I'm going to invite you to join her."*

Living Like Mary, or Martha?

As you think through the picture of these two sisters, ask yourself some questions . . . and answer honestly:

Which sister do I more closely resemble?
Have I chosen the good part, as Mary did?
Have I put myself at Jesus' feet, living in subjection to Him?
Am I listening to His Word and doing what He says?
Am I keeping my life in proper perspective, understanding what is really important and what is not?
Am I letting insignificant things upset my apple cart?

Living with the Lord's peace, joy, and power truly is a choice we can make. You and I can experience the wonderful fruit of the Spirit as we choose to yield to Jesus Christ in every area of life. God is not asking us to grit our teeth and somehow manufacture a smile and "fake it until we make it." He is asking us to simply choose to put our lives at His feet, as "a living and holy sacrifice, acceptable to God" (Rom. 12:1). As we do, He provides all that we need to live life to the full, overcoming even the worst of circumstances.

The Prince of Peace

One of the wonderful names of Jesus is Prince of Peace (Isa. 9:6). He came to give us peace *with* God, which He provided when He died for our sins and rose again from the dead. He also came to give us the peace *of* God, which He offers to all who will make the choice to enthrone Him as King and Lord of all.

How can you tell if Jesus is really your Lord? Honestly answer this simple question: Is there peace in your heart right now? If not, you have followed in Martha's footsteps and derailed. But the good news is, you don't have to stay derailed. You can choose the good part, just as Mary did. You can make up your mind to trace the smoke alarm back to the source of the fire and deal with the flames head-on. You can have a life filled with the good things of God as you choose His will and His ways.

The choice really is yours. Don't go another minute living worried, bothered, and on fire. Put the truths of this book into practice, and see God do a miracle in you!

NOTES

Introduction

1. "Spock – Fascinating!" YouTube.com, uploaded on July 31, 2009, http://www.youtube.com/watch?v=cFods1KSWsQ.
2. "Wise Jan Hammer Quotes," *Jonathan Lockwood Huie's Words of Wisdom Quotes*, accessed December 10, 2012, http://www.inspirational-wisdom-quotes.com/by/jan-hammer.

Chapter 1

1. *The Lion King*, LionKing.org, accessed December 10, 2012, *http://www.lionking.org/scripts/Script.html*.
2. "His Vocabulary Was Inadequate," Dr. Adrian Rogers, http://www.baptistfire.com/gospel/lee.shtml, (site discontinued).

Chapter 2

1. "Mother Teresa saw loneliness as leprosy of the West," *The News Times*, published April 17, 2004, *http://www.newstimes.com/news/article/Mother-Teresa-saw-loneliness-as-leprosy-of-the-250607.php*.
2. "Gilbert O'Sullivan--Alone Again (original version)," YouTube.com, uploaded August 18, 2006, http://www.youtube.com/watch?v=D_P-v1BVQn8.
3. "Alone Again (Naturally) lyrics," LyricsMode.com, accessed December 10, 2012, http://www.lyricsmode.com/lyrics/g/gilbert_osullivan/alone_again_naturally.html.
4. "Loneliness Quotes: Famous Quotes about Loneliness from *All the Best Quotes*," Chatna.com, accessed December 10, 2012, http://chatna.com/theme/loneliness.htm.
5. "Quotation of Orson Welles," Dictionary.com Quotes, accessed December 11, 2012, http://quotes.dictionary.com/Were_born_alone_we_live_alone_we_die.

6. "Eleanor Rigby by The Beatles," *Observer Music Monthly*, November 2008, http://www.songfacts.com/detail.php?id=102.

7. "Selah," Dictionary.com, accessed December 5, 2012, http://dictionary.reference.com/browse/selah?s=t.

8. "Hebrews 13:5," Biblos.com, accessed December 1, 2012, *http://biblos .com/hebrews/13-5.htm.*

9. "Lexicon Results," *Blue Letter Bible*, accessed November 28, 2012, *http://www.blueletterbible.org/lang/lexicon/lexicon.cfm?Strongs =G1632&t=NASB.*

10. "Poor Poor Pitiful Me," *The Very Best of Linda Ronstadt*, http://www .ronstadt-linda.com/simple.htm#poor.

CHAPTER 3

1. "Nowhere Man," SongFacts.com, accessed November 25, 2012, http://www.songfacts.com/detail.php?id=88.

2. Ibid.

3. Henry Blackaby, Richard Blackaby, and Claude King, *Experiencing God: Knowing and Doing the Will of God, Revised and Expanded* (Nashville: B & H Publishing Group, 2008), 302.

CHAPTER 4

1. "Worry affects the circulation . . ." QuoteWorld.org, accessed December 11, 2012, *http://www.quoteworld.org/quotes/8804.*

2. "The beginning of anxiety . . ." QuotationsBook.com, accessed December 11, 2012, http://quotationsbook.com/quote/14000.

3. *The Ten Commandments*, directed by Cecil DeMille (1956; Hollywood, CA: Paramount Pictures).

4. "One of God's Great Don'ts," *Daily Devotionals* by Oswald Chambers, posted July 4, 2012,, http://utmost.org/classic/one-of-god%E2%80 %99s-great-don%E2%80%99ts-classic.

5. "Veggie Tales (Veggie Tunes) 'My God is So Big,'"SongLyrics.com, accessed November 28, 2012, http://www.songlyrics.com/veggie -tales-veggie-tunes/my-god-is-so-big-lyrics.

6. "Worry – Finding That Eight Percent!" *The Expository Files*, accessed December 8, 2012, www.bible.ca/ef/topical-worry-finding-that-eight -percent.htm.

7. Tony Evans, *Tony Evans' Book of Illustrations: Stories, Quotes, and Anecdotes From More Than 30 Years of Preaching and Public Speaking* (Chicago, IL: Moody Publishers, 2009), 311.

CHAPTER 5

1. "George Carlin quotes," ThinkExist.com, accessed December 8, 2012, http://thinkexist.com/quotation/have_you_ever_noticed_that _anybody_driving_slower/207686.html.
2. "What is Forgiveness?", *Walk in the Word*, accessed December 3, 2012, http://www.walkintheword.com/WeeklyWalk.aspx.

CHAPTER 6

1. William Shakespeare, *Macbeth*, act 5, scene 1 (New York, NY: Oxford University Press, 2nd ed, 2005).
2. "Juvenal Quotes," ThinkExist.com, accessed December 12, 2012, http://en.thinkexist.com/quotes/Juvenal.
3. "Confessions That Will Change Your Life," Brewster Baptist Church Sermon Archive, posted March 29, 2009, http://www .brewsterbaptistchurch.org/sermon_archive/2009/03.29.09.pdf.
4. "Psychology is Unspiritual," *African Aquatics*, accessed December 12, 2012, http://www.africanaquatics.co.za/_christian/_articles/psychology .htm.

CHAPTER 7

1. "Martin Luther Quotes," ThinkExist.com, accessed December 12, 2012, www.thinkexist.com.
2. Extreme Devotion Writing Team (editor), *Extreme Devotion: The Voice of the Martyrs* (Nashville, TN: Thomas Nelson, 2001), 218.

CHAPTER 8

1. Joseph Bayly, *Psalms of My Life* (Colorado Springs, CO: Cook Communications Ministries Intl., 2000).
2. "Depression," *Sermon Illustrations,* accessed December 12, 2012, www.sermonillustrations.com.
3. Charles Haddon Spurgeon, *Lectures to My Students* (Grand Rapids, MI: Zondervan, 1979), 249.
4. Abraham Lincoln, "The Writings of Abraham Lincoln," *The Classic Literature Library*, accessed December 12, 2012, http://www.classic -literature.co.uk.
5. Wayne Cordeiro, *Leading on Empty: Refilling Your Tank and Renewing Your Passion* (Ada, MI: Bethany House Publishers, 2010).
6. "Three Tips for Raising Grateful Teens," *Menninger,* accessed December 12, 2012, http://www.menningerclinic.com/about /newsroom/recent-news/three-tips-for-raising-grateful-teens.